TIME WITHOUT KEYS

Selected Poems

Photograph of Ida Vitale taken by her daughter, Amparo Rama

TIME WITHOUT KEYS

Selected Poems

Ida Vitale

Translated from the Spanish by Sarah Pollack

A New Directions Paperbook Original

The six poems from Vitale's collection Listener Errant were first published in Reason Enough, translated by Sarah Pollack (Host Publications, 2007). Thanks to Host Publications for permission to reproduce these poems, some with slight revisions.

Manufactured in the United States of America
First published as a New Directions Paperbook (NDP 1572) in 2023
Design by Marian Bantjes

Library of Congress Cataloging-in-Publication Data
Names: Vitale, Ida, author. | Pollack, Sarah, 1976- translator. | Vitale, Ida. Time without keys (2023) | Vitale, Ida. Time without keys. Spanish (2023)
Title: Time without keys : selected poems / Ida Vitale ; translated from the Spanish by Sarah Pollack.
Other titles: Time without keys (Compilation (2023))
Description: New York, NY : New Directions Publishing Corporation, 2023.
Identifiers: LCCN 2023016500 | ISBN 9780811231923 (paperback) | ISBN 9780811231930 (ebook)
Subjects: LCSH: Vitale, Ida—Translations into English. | LCGFT: Poetry.
Classification: LCC PQ8519.V72 T5613 2023 | DDC 861/.64—dc23/eng/20230511
LC record available at https://lccn.loc.gov/2023016500

10 9 8 7 6 5 4 3 2 1

New Directions Books are published for James Laughlin
by New Directions Publishing Corporation
80 Eighth Avenue, New York 10011
ndbooks.com

Contents

from Time Without Keys / Tiempo sin claves (2021)

3 Devices
3 The Big Question
5 Vegetate
5 Too Late
7 Recalcitrant
9 Falconry
9 Natural Leaves
11 Photo with Little Paper Bird
13 A Painter Reflects
17 Dream in the Nudist Colony
19 Iceland, 2000
21 Nostalgia for the Dodo
23 Between Yeses and Noes
23 Without the Name of the Bird
25 Plea

from Specks of Freezing Rain / Mínimas de aguanieve (2015)

27 As Go the Birds
31 Blind the Light
31 Nell'ora credula
33 Fragile Colors
35 Vestiges

from Chip and Sift / Mella y criba (2010)

39 History Lesson
41 Austin
43 Triangular Relationships
45 Demented Alliances
45 High Bough

47 Mockingbird and Daisies
49 Summer Gratitude
51 My Tribute
53 Book
55 Name in the Wind
57 A Very Vicious Circle
59 Program

from Trema / Trema (2005)
61 Sea of Doubt
61 Platform
63 Fortune
65 New Certainties
65 Closure
67 Dead Grackle
69 Merry-Go-Round
71 In the Dark Entryway
73 New Obligations
73 In the Air
75 Possible Explanation

from Reduction of the Infinite / Reducción del infinito (2002)
77 So-Called Life
79 Vortex
79 A Culture of Palimpsest
81 Parentheses, Fragile Shelter
83 To Translate
85 Sums
87 Droplets
87 Autumn
89 Patrimony
91 Trees
93 Annunciation

95   The Glory of Philitis

97   Starling

99   Snail

from Search for the Impossible / Procura de lo imposible (1998)

101   The Mockingbird Series

105   Montevideo

107   Set the Blackbird Free

109   Pigeon

109   March

111   Image of the Floating World

113   Calendar

115   Clinamen

117   Exiles

119   Sicily

121   To Octavio Paz

123   Quotidian

from Dictionary of Affinities / Léxico de afinidades (1994)

125   Anaphoric

125   Syllable

127   Hamlet (News for)

127   Saxifrage

129   Dream

131   Unicorn

from Dreams of Constancy / Sueños de la constancia (1984)

133   Tiny Kingdom

137   A Meadow for Orpheus

139   Dark

141   From Tiger the Leap

143   We Left an Angel

145   Not Saying, Talking, Talking

from Garden of Silica / Jardín de sílice (1980)

 147 Summer

 149 Garden of Silica

 151 Drought

from Listener Errant / Oidor andante (1972)

 151 The Word

 153 Nocturnal War

 153 Backroom

 155 Woman with Dog

 157 History Is Not Forgotten

 159 Chapter

from Each in His Night / Cada uno en su noche (1960)

 161 This World

 163 Step by Step

 165 Finale of the Phoenix

from Given Word / Palabra dada (1953)

 167 Encounter and Loss

 169 Furtherlife

from The Light of This Memory / La luz de esta memoria (1949)

 171 Night, This Dwelling

 174 Poems in Search of the Initiated: An Essay

 176 Translator's Afterword

TIME WITHOUT KEYS

Selected Poems

Recursos

El sobresalto fuera del poema y dentro del poema, apenas aire contenido.

Leer y releer una frase, una palabra, un rostro. Los rostros, sobre todo.
Repasar, pesar bien lo que callan.

Como no estás a salvo de nada, intenta ser tú mismo la salvación de algo.

Caminar despacio, a ver si, tentado el tiempo, hace lo mismo.

La gran pregunta

¿Qué hacer? ¿Abrir al mar la estancia de la muerte? ¿O enterrarse entre piedras que encierran amonitas fantasmas y prueban que fue agua este humano desierto?

Devices

Startled outside the poem and within the poem, air scarcely contained.

Read and reread a sentence, a word, a face. Faces, above all. Revisit, weigh their silences with care.

As you're safe from nothing, try being the salvation of something yourself.

Walk slowly, to see if, time is tempted, to do the same.

The Big Question

What to do? Open death's abode to the sea? Or inter oneself among rocks enclosing ghostly ammonites that prove this human wasteland was once water?

Vegetar

¿Será tan malo vegetar? ¿Habrá que echar raíces, con la permanencia que eso implica? Quizás baste un poco de arena, pero entonces será un cacto lo que venga a nuevo estado. Sin duda será mejor buscar para la experiencia un poco de buena tierra negra, porque tampoco cualquier tierra se presta para la aventura que comienza. ¿Serán suficientes unos brotes? Pero por más que uno se ponga voluntarista, aquéllos no van a aparecer por ningún lado si no logra una mínima raíz. Y para esto se necesita quietud. ¿Hundimiento y quietud?

Demasiado tarde

Lo que el verano nos quita, el lugar que el verano nos deja, el don del estornino, su ir y venir ansioso entre su sala de pastos, ¿su selva?, su desaparecer—¿hacia dónde?— con su verdoso salpicado de oro, si el viento de pronto se levanta, si aquella nube, para nada esperada, gotea.

Vegetate

Can vegetating be so bad? Must you take root, with the permanence that implies? Perhaps a little sand would suffice, but then it would be a cactus that achieves a new state. Doubtless, it would be better to seek some black earth for the experience, as not just any soil is apt for the adventure that begins. Are a few sprouts enough? But no matter how willful you are, they'll emerge nowhere without minimal roots. And for this you need stillness. Sinking and stillness?

Too Late

What summer takes from us, the place summer leaves behind for us, the starling's gift, its eager coming and going from its parlor of grasses, (its jungle?), its disappearance —whereto?— with its greenish splash of gold, if the wind suddenly picks up, if that unforeseen cloud drips.

Renuente

Después de los ochenta,
rechazarás el azafrán y el chile,
desde siempre las innobles sandías,
las mentiras del arte del falsario.

Dejarán de angustiarte
las teorías estéticas,
la maldad del azúcar,
el ego, las historias
que la gente se inventa
para alegrar el suyo,
la inabarcable gira
de ajenas cacerías.

Mira las piedras y las hojas,
umbrales de la paz,
sin olvidar que
sobre el descuido
alguien aguarda tu caída inerte.

Recalcitrant

After eighty,
you won't stomach saffron or chili,
having always rejected ignoble watermelon,
the lies of the artful deceiver.

You'll no longer be troubled
by aesthetic theories,
the evils of sugar,
or the ego, the tales
people invent
to cheer themselves up,
or the measureless journey
of others' pursuits.

Observe stones and leaves,
thresholds of peace,
never forgetting that
above carelessness hangs
someone who awaits your motionless fall.

Cetrería

Anda perdida una palabra
como un pájaro joven, sin nido aún,
sin centro ni alegación
ni encanto donde caer,
ni nociones del bien o el mal,
apenas un instinto todavía dormido.
Me pregunto:
     ¿dónde el alpiste de atraer palabras?
     ¿dónde la liga que las detenga, sin herirlas?
     Y luego, ¿cómo hacerlas vivir en lo precario?

Hojas naturales

… o el arraigo, escribir en un espacio idéntico
siempre, casa o desvío.
       —José M. Algaba

Arrastro por los cambios un lápiz,
una hoja, tan sólo de papel, que quisiera
como de árbol, vivaz y renaciente,
que destilase savia y no inútil tristeza
y no fragilidad, disoluciones;
una hoja que fuese alucinada, autónoma,
capaz de iluminarme, llevándome
al pasado por una ruta honesta: abiertas
las paredes cegadas y limpia
la historia verdadera de las pintarrajeadas
artimañas que triunfan.
Hoja y lápiz, para un oído limpio,
curioso y desconfiado.

Falconry

A word is wandering around lost
like a young bird, without a nest yet,
without center or argument
or spell on which to land,
without notions of good or evil,
only a still sleeping instinct.
I ask myself:
> Where is the seed to attract words?
> The glue to trap them, without harming them?
> And then, how to make them live in such precariousness?

Natural Leaves

> ... or be rooted, writing in an identical space
> always, a home or detour.
> —José M. Algaba

I drag a pencil across the changes,
a leaf, only of paper, that I wish
were like those of a tree, perennial and renascent,
distilling sap, not futile sadness,
not fragility, dissolutions;
a hallucinated, autonomous leaf,
able to illuminate me, guide me
to the past down an honest path: blinded
walls open and the true history clear
of the scribbled
tricks that triumph.
Leaf and pencil, for a clear,
inquisitive and wary ear.

Foto con pajarita de papel

Para Daniel Mordzinski

Entonces vino a mi mano
que sin labor se engreía,
para la fotografía,
extravagante y expresa
de Daniel, la gran sorpresa
que instantánea me depara,
esa pajarita rara,
solución harto inventiva,
a la que acompaño viva
y hacia mi muerte la gano.
Origami milagreado,
leve papel ojeroso,
recortado, osteoporoso,
cosa sin hueso que danza,
y escapando a la balanza
que no lo pesa, procura
llegar flotando a la altura
para volar con el viento,
como un pájaro entre ciento,
sin canto pero encantado.

Photo with Little Paper Bird

for Daniel Mordzinski

And then it landed in my hand
that labored not for such conceits,
for the extravagant and fleet
photo taken by Daniel,
a great surprise for me as well
as instantaneously emerged
such a rare little bird,
quite an inventive solution
to earn near death's conclusion
and whom in life I accompany.
Miraculous origami,
paper feather-light, insomnious,
jagged cutout, osteoporous,
this boneless thing that dances,
eluding thus the balance
undetected, it contrives
to float above to great heights
and fly through wind unbounded,
like one bird among one hundred,
without songs but still enchanted.

Un pintor reflexiona

Qué pocas cosas tiene
este callado mundo,
más allá de mis Cosas.
Está ese sol que incendia
las paredes vecinas,
los cables del tendido
y aquí no entra porque
¿qué pensaría el triste,
el alón del sombrero
que, perdida su copa,
ya no abandona el muro
y tengo por la Elipse?
Y las flores de trapo,
que pintadas soñaron
con ser frescas y hermosas
y sobreviven mustias,
¿qué dirían, mis eternas?
Mis ocres, lilas, rosas,
mis marfiles sesgados
por sombras que entretejen
mis líneas adivinas,
son, en su quieto reino.
No importa el sol, afuera.
Que le baste Bolonia
y el ladrillo ardoroso
y en mera luz y sombras
me deje entre mis Cosas.
Ya nos encontraremos
si en el pequeño parque,
pinto y pienso en Corot.

A Painter Reflects

How few are the things
this hushed world has,
beyond my own Things.
There's that sun setting fire
to the neighboring walls,
the electric lines,
which doesn't enter here because
what would the poor
brim of my hat think,
never leaving its wall
after losing its crown,
and that I take to be the Ellipse?
And the cloth flowers,
which once painted, dreamed
of being fresh and beautiful,
and survive, wilted,
what would you say, my eternal ones?
My ochres, lilacs, rosy pinks,
my marbles skewed
by shadows that interweave
with my divining lines,
exist, in their motionless realm.
The sun doesn't matter, outside.
May Bologna
and burning bricks suffice
and in mere light and shadow
leave me among my Things.
We'll meet again
if in the small park
I paint and think about Corot.

Voy a ser aún más leve:
en leves acuarelas
últimas, que precisen
el paso de las formas
por la bruma que sea
un color suficiente.
Pintaré un mandolino
que acompañe la danza
de mis disposiciones
entre sí con sus sombras,
con luces y con trazos
que sutiles abrazan
mis objetos amados.
Y ya toda Bolonia
será de un suaverrosa
sin presunción alguna,
sobre el hastío fatal
y sí, decimonónico,
de lecheras y henares,
gallineros y cielos.
Cerca de mis hermanas,
viajaré por mis Cosas.

I'll be fainter still:
in faint watercolors,
my last, that require
the passage of forms
through the mist
to be color enough.
I'll paint a mandolin
to accompany the dance
of my dispositions
with each other and their shadows,
with lights and lines
that subtly embrace
my beloved objects.
And then all Bologna
will turn a gentlerose
with no suspicion
of the inevitable ennui,
very nineteenth-century, indeed,
of milkmaids and hayfields,
henhouses and skies.
Close to my sisters,
I will travel through my Things.

Sueño en el campo nudista

En Jungborn, en el Harz,
hay colinas y un prado,
y en lo verde, cabañas.
Con cautela, Kafka abre la puerta de la suya.
No le agrada la idea de ver aproximarse
algún cuerpo desnudo
de los que a veces pasan.
Bajo la poca luz, hay tres conejos
que lo miran, quietos.
¿Adustos? Vienen quizás a reclamarle,
a él, que está vestido, la intromisión
de lo innatural en lo natural:
gente desnuda junto a castos conejos,
arropados en su pelaje suave,
"variegati" diríamos, si ellos fuesen
tres plantas que han optado por moverse,
pero por un segundo estarán quietas.
El aterrado Kafka olvida sus pulmones
y entra a soñar mi sueño.

Dream in the Nudist Colony

In Jungborn, in the Harz,
there are hills and a meadow,
and on the green, cabins.
Cautiously, Kafka opens the door to his.
He loathes the idea of seeing
a nude body approach
among those that sometimes pass by.
In the dim light, three rabbits
observe him, unmoving.
Sternly? They've come, perhaps, to remonstrate
him, who is clothed, for the intrusion
of the unnatural in the natural:
nude people alongside chaste rabbits,
swathed in their soft fur,
"variegated," we'd say, if they were
three plants that have opted for motion,
but for a second remain still.
Kafka, terrified, forgets his lungs
and steps in to dream my dream.

Islandia, 2000

Ceibos, ceibas, solamente una letra
marca la clara diferencia.
Rojos ceibos y verdes ceibas reinan,
como saúcos, sauces y cipreses,
en la dichosa incandescencia usual
de un sur lleno de cantos y colores.
En Islandia, la isla azul y blanca,
no hay pájaros, tan solo aves marinas,
ningún canto, pero solo el de las manos,
manos que mueven no todas las piedras
para que el musgo nazca y el verde
empiece a cantar, entonces suave.

* "No todas," porque las que pueden ser casa de un elfo, en los que muchos creen, se respetan.

Iceland, 2000

Ceibos, ceibas, only one letter
marks their clear distinction.
Red ceibos and green ceibas reign,
also elderberries, willows, and cypresses,
in the blessed incandescence
common in the south awash with songs and colors.
In Iceland, the blue and white island,
there are no songbirds, only seabirds,
no music, except that of hands,
hands moving stones, but not every stone,
so moss can grow and the green
can begin singing, ever softly.

* Author's note: "Not every stone," because those that could be a home to an elf, which
many believe in, are respected.

Nostalgia del dodó

Tengo nostalgia del dodó.
No extraño algo ficticio, casi un mito,
aunque se olviden de él los diccionarios.
Surgió tan real como vejez y muerte,
él en una vitrina del Victoria
y Alberto, yo asombrada de su existir
fuera de las lecturas de la infancia,
inmensa compañía inocente,
del conejo vestido y de su prisa.

Parecido a una oca, no le valió
el agresivo pico, para salvar
de la extinción su simpática raza
en un tiempo salvaje, quizás peor,
que no me hubiese gustado conocer.
Imaginé la blancura de un cisne
en sus plumas, marfil añejo ahora,
de piano abandonado o de encajes
de venerables bodas. Imaginé
su raro andar a partir de sus tarsos,
desasistido guardián de una verdad
que se volvió fantasía difusa.

Sí, tengo nostalgia del dodó, y más,
de tantas extinciones que él resume,
de ese tiempo de cruzar los espejos
y descubrir que el mal podía
abolirse, no ser más que una absurda
figura que escapó de una baraja.

Nostalgia for the Dodo

I'm nostalgic for the dodo.
What I miss isn't fictional, almost a myth,
even if dictionaries do forget it.
It appeared as real as old age and death,
in a display case at the Victoria
and Albert, astonishing me with its existence
beyond my childhood readings,
the immense and innocent companion
of the waistcoated rabbit and his haste.

Akin to a goose, its aggressive beak
was of no use to save its sympathetic
race from extinction during a time
of savagery, maybe worse,
when I wouldn't have wished to live.
I imagined its feathers swan
white, now the yellowed ivory
of abandoned pianos or lace
from a venerable wedding. I imagined
its strange tarsal gait,
the deserted guardian of a truth
transformed into dim fantasy.

Yes, I'm nostalgic for the dodo, and more,
for the countless extinctions it condenses,
for the time of crossing the looking-glass
to discover that evil could be
vanquished, being nothing but an absurd
figure escaped from a deck of cards.

Entre síes y noes

En el principio fui dulce, fui obediente,
descubrí luego hartos motivos para el no.
Luego, mucho, mucho después
fue posible el sí sometido al amor,
la confianza ganada entre paredes fieles.
Pero, arco triste, a solas ya, decae.
Fuera de las ventanas y a lo lejos,
ofrece el no sus afilados dientes
a lo obtuso del mundo y sus conjuras.

Sin el nombre del pájaro

Qué desolado ese piar en medio
de esta lluvia nocturna que anticipa el relámpago
y el rodar poderoso del trueno que lo sigue.
No tiene nido o ha perdido el rumbo.
Qué soledad, como de ser sin alma
o con más alma de la conveniente.
Alguien un día estará solo, oyendo
esta misma tristeza y este canto,
disperso entonces lo hoy entrelazado.

Between Yeses and Noes

In the beginning I was sweet, obedient.
I later discovered a surfeit of motives for No.
Then later, much, much later,
Yes was possible, when harnessed to love,
to trust earned within faithful walls.
But, unhappy arc, alone now, Yes decays.
Outside the windows and from a distance,
No bares its sharpened teeth
at the world's obtuseness and its conspiracies.

Without the Name of the Bird

How desolate that chirping in the midst
of this nocturnal rain before each lightning flash
and the powerful roll of thunder that follows.
It has no nest or has lost its way.
What loneliness, like being soulless
or with more soul than is prudent.
One day somebody will be alone, listening
to this same sadness and this song,
scattered when now so interwoven.

Ruego

El Paraíso, ¿acaso el paraíso?
Un paraíso de árboles y cielo
—pero en el cielo ¿cómo ver el Cielo?—,
y un árbol con sus frutos—no manzanas,
que, sabiamente, nunca me tentaron—
peras y uvas (me olvido de Noé).
Paraíso: la paz pero sin tedio,
el descanso deseado, mas deseante,
algún leve deber, no el ocio/hastío.
Por allí no se aceptan animales,
ni una triste tortuga, solitaria,
en aburridas invernadas, sabia.
¿Y un perrito pequeño sin pecado?
Los perritos enseñan la constancia,
quizás enseñan a morir en calma,
eso a esa altura inútil, obviamente.
Caminando sin prisa, sin dolores,
Confucio, que no buscó el poder,
podría ayudar a organizar las cosas ...

El Paraíso, ¿acaso el paraíso?
No te olvides, Señor, del Paraíso.
Aquí en un tiempo nos gustaba mucho.

Plea

Is Paradise really a paradise?
A paradise of trees and sky
—but in the sky, how does one see Heaven?—
and a tree laden with fruit—not apples,
which, wisely, never tempted me—
pears and grapes (I forget about Noah).
Paradise: peace, not tedium,
desired rest, but desirous,
some light chores, not leisure/languor.
Animals aren't allowed there,
not even a sad turtle, solitary,
in tedious hibernation, sage.
How about a small, sinless dog?
Dogs teach constancy,
perhaps how to die in peace,
which is useless at this point, obviously.
Walking without haste, without pain,
Confucius, who never sought power,
could help organize things …

Is Paradise really a paradise?
Don't forget, Lord, your Paradise.
Here at one time we liked it so much.

Va de pájaros

Tanti gridi di passeri,
Tante danze nei rami ...
—Giuseppi Ungaretti

En el árbol, el pájaro
canta a solas su miedo
de estar solo.

Con el trino de un pájaro
vuelven dos a ser uno.

Torcazas:
    esponjados arrullos
que desgajan augurios
desde la altura.

Para la rosa,
telón donde enmarcar
su renovado renacer,
la nube oscura.

El pájaro preluce
a contraluz, en vuelo,
el comienzo del canto.
La noche dicta el fin.

Prendió el fuego en los árboles,
recorrió llama a llama
la materia más muerta.
Salvó el pájaro el canto
en lo aún verde del bosque,
pulcramente limpiándolo

As Go the Birds

So many cries of sparrows,
So many dances in the boughs ...
                    —Giuseppi Ungaretti (tr. Patrick Creagh)

In the tree, the bird
sings a solo about his fear
of solitude.

With the trill of a bird
two become one again.

Eared doves:
        airy coos
that break the news
from the heights.

For the rose,
the backdrop framing
its renewed rebirth:
a dark cloud.

The bird gives
in counterlight, in flight,
the beginning of song.
Night dictates the end.

Fire ignited in the trees,
sweeping flame to flame
the deadest matter.
The bird safeguarded song
in the ever green of the forest,
carefully cleansing it

de crujido y ceniza,
dándole sitio al aire.

Profundamente pájaro,
profundamente río,
profundamente cielo
y árboles y árboles
profundos y distintos,
marejada de nubes sobre
golondrinas, cotorras,
palomas, benteveos
y constantes gorriones
y remilgados teros,
silencios con abrojos,
errores tan fatales,
imprecisas historias
de miserias ¿humanas?

¿Qué traman los lustrosos estorninos
en círculo, en el centro de un paisaje
no adecuado quizás a este mensaje
de inquietud hecho y de pocos trinos?

of crackles and ash,
making space for the air.

Deeply bird,
deeply river,
deeply sky
and trees and more trees,
each deep and different
swells of clouds above
swallows, parakeets,
pigeons, kiskadees
and constant sparrows
and finicky lapwings,
thistle-filled silences,
mistakes so fatal,
inexact histories
of (humankind's?) miseries.

What are the lustrous starlings scheming
while circling in the center of this scene
incompatible perhaps with this theme
composed of trepidation and scant warbling?

Cegar la luz

Desagradezco días degradados.
Amanecimos mal, el día y yo.
Pueden llover desgracias,
aunque no sepa cuáles.
Con un cierto pavor,
ruego por menos luz,
que sábanas me cubran
y alejen la ciénaga que traga.
La aceptaré otro día
pero no hoy, hoy no.

Nell'ora credula

Entré en la tarde
por donde no debía y la sorprendo
en el ritual para abrir el otoño:
quizás aún son amarillos
los naranjas, no alcanzaron
los rojos un matiz amaranto
y sorprendentes verdes brotan,
distraído rezago.
Debo olvidar los pequeños errores,
volver por donde vine a la paciencia,
corregir mi reloj, único errado.

Blind the Light

I decry degraded days.
We rose amiss, the day and I.
Misfortunes may rain down,
though I don't know which ones.
With certain dread,
I plead for less light,
for sheets to cover me
and keep the devouring morass at bay.
I'll welcome it another day
but not today, today no.

Nell'ora credula

I stepped into the afternoon
where I shouldn't be and startle her
in the ritual of unfurling autumn:
perhaps the oranges are still
yellow, the reds have not yet reached
the shade of amaranth,
and surprising greens sprout,
distracted holdovers.
I should forget these small mistakes,
return the way I came to patience,
reset my clock, the only one mistaken.

* Translator's note: The title of this poem ("In the Credulous Hour") is from a line in
   Giuseppe Ungaretti's poem "Canzone."

Colores frágiles

Decimos verde agua,
¿qué agua, de qué vaso?
Hoy este río es verde,
profundo verde de árbol,
verde o azul, de pájaro
o piedras más o menos preciosas.
Pero otro día es torvo,
como se puso aquella
mirada hacia la tarde
y piensas en la rara
fragilidad del gozo
y en la escapularia
protección que persigues.

Fragile Colors

We say green water,
but what water, in what glass?
Today this river is green,
deep tree green,
green or blue, of a bird
or stones more or less precious.
But another day it is sinister,
like that look transformed
toward evening
and you ponder pleasure's
strange fragility
and the scapular
protection you pursue.

Vestigios

1

El grillo sin engaños
ensarta perfumes en su aguja,
en la noche los alza.

2

Desde un colchón de nubes
un gato blanco salta
a las ramas de un árbol:
luna amistosa.

3

A través de la niebla
pasa un llamado
que no se llena de alas doradas
y que no colman
palabras vagas.

4

El árbol no cede
una hoja gustoso.
Sabe que lejos de él
sólo será hoja seca.

5

En las ciudades,
los gallos llegan en jirones.

6

Los caracoles bordan
sobre el pasto
su pretensión de lujo.

Vestiges

1
The guileless cricket
threads perfumes in his needle,
raising them by night.

2
From a cloud cushion
a white cat leaps
to the boughs of a tree:
amicable moon.

3
Through the fog
a call rings out
not filled with golden wings
and not fulfilled by
idle words.

4
The tree doesn't surrender
a leaf willingly.
He knows that far from him
only dried leaves exist.

5
In the cities,
roosters arrive in tatters.

6
Snails embroider
the grass
with ambitions of luxury.

7
No respiran los pájaros:
por su canto respira el mundo.

8
Y no canta el jazmín;
su perfume es la endecha
que hacia el aire traslada.

9
Muere la muerte:
el fin de la semana
se suspende el trajín.

10
Un destino posible:
irse, sobrando.
De la nada a la nada.

7
Birds do not breathe:
their song is the breath of the world.

8
And jasmine does not sing;
its perfume is the dirge
translated for the air.

9
Death is dying:
at the week's end
the hustle comes to a halt.

10
A possible fate:
leave, being left over.
From nothing to nothingness.

Lección de historia

Que una moneda antigua,
hallada—¿por azar?—en el jardín,
te enseñara una fecha: 1804
y un dato no ficticio:
Napoleón rey de Italia,
importó menos que,
abierto el campo
de ilusa fantasía,
luego de la lección de cosas,
el bronce atesorado
se disipara sin palabras.

Quedó en el aire
algo de Historia y Algo
todavía sin nombre:
un comienzo, la insana
costumbre de observar,
atar cabos, alcanzar
la no errada visión
de algún prójimo horrible.

Saber que nada es tuyo
para siempre.

History Lesson

That an old coin,
found—by chance?—in the garden
taught you a date: 1804
and a fact not untrue:
Napoleon King of Italy,
mattered less than
—the realm of illusive
fantasy now open,
after this lesson about things—
the treasured bronze's
wordless disappearance.

Something about History
hung in the air and Something
still unnamed:
a beginning, the unhealthy
habit of observing,
connecting the dots, reaching
an unmistaken conception
of one's horrible fellow man.

Knowing that nothing is yours
forever.

Austin

El pensamiento va
de una casa a los árboles,
se detiene en un pájaro.
Una esquina, una nariz extraña
se funden y alejan el rayo de luz,
las graves, interiores inercias.

Todo es suma de partes:
debería aprender cuáles forman
esto que avanza
o retrocede inescrutable
por la ajena ciudad que me ha aceptado
en sus misterios inasibles:
distancias aun no sumadas y tatuajes,
pocos susurros, arrebatos dementes,
prescindibles noticias aventadas
al oído en que caigan,
algo vago que reemplaza las almas.

Un enclave muy íntimo
se duele de la huella del monstruo
en el camino que nadie cree seguir
y yo sospecho.
Esa quimera de lucidez es
vago consuelo
para un itinerario ciego.

Austin

Thought flits
from a house to the trees,
pausing on a bird.
A street corner, a strange nose
merge and dispel the ray of light,
the grave, inner inertias.

Everything is the sum of parts:
I must learn which ones make up
this inscrutable thing
that advances or recedes
through this alien city that has let me in
on its elusive mysteries:
distances that still don't add up and tattoos,
scant whispers, fits of madness,
dispensable news hurled
and falling on random ears,
something vague replacing souls.

An intimate enclave
aches from the monster's footprint
on the path no one intends to follow
and I suspect.
That chimera of lucidity is
dim consolation
for a blind itinerary.

Relaciones triangulares

Hace un rato
que en la encina cercana
protesta un grajo.
Mi vecina, la gata
blanquinegra e inaudible,
asoma en la ventana.
Mira al árbol
y encerrada imagina
la aventura riesgosa.
Mira al grajo y me mira.
No sabe a quién apoyo.
Para alguien que no existe
un raro trío hacemos
en tres lenguas distintas,
dos silencios y el ruido
del grajo inaccesible.

Triangular Relationships

For a while now
a grackle has been protesting
in the nearby oak.
My neighbor, the cat
—black-and-white and inaudible—
looks at the tree
from the window.
Captive, she imagines
the perilous adventure.
She looks at the grackle and looks at me,
not knowing whom I support.
For someone who doesn't exist
we make a strange trio
in three different languages,
two silences and the noise
of the unattainable grackle.

Alianzas dementes

El grajo busca al hombre,
confía en sus manjares,
acepta las dañosas ofertas
y devora con breve cuerpo
los venenos que encuentra,
pingües constelaciones
de males del futuro
en dulces o saladas bazofias.
Sus artejos torcidos,
sus patas mutiladas,
sus formas que eran sabias
son gorjeos de muerte.
Ignora que la humana libertad
relativa tiene el gusto suicida
por pluma de sus alas.

Vara alta

Vara alta de plátano falso
desde sus hojas firmemente aferradas,
lejana, mira los blancos plumones que caen,
hacia el sueño que trepa los límites
de sus pocos recursos terrestres.
Su rumor, ¿dice la música del tiempo que pasa
en la gruta en donde aparecen figuras ideales?
Es la fuente que brinda,
entre silencios asombrados,
silenciosas promesas cumplidas
cada día, cada día.

Demented Alliances

The grackle seeks man out,
has faith in his delicacies,
accepts harmful offerings,
devouring with his brief body
the poisons that he discovers,
fat constellations
of future maladies
made of sweet or salty scraps.
His gnarled knuckles,
his mutilated feet,
his ways that were wise
become death warbles.
He is unaware that relative
human freedom has a suicidal taste
for feathers from his wings.

High Bough

High bough of the sycamore maple,
from its closely clinging leaves,
far away, it watches as white down drops
toward the dream that scales the limits
of its few earthly resources.
Does its murmur speak the music of time passing
in the cave where ideal figures appear?
It is the fountain that affords,
between astonished silences,
silent promises fulfilled
every day, every day.

Translator's note: Opening line in italics is from Enrique Fierro's poem "Memorial."

Sinsonte y margaritas

De nuevo aquí el sinsonte,
el ruiseñor del día,
acróbata por los aires de plata.
De nuevo es marzo,
para él feliz, y danza
y en ese impulso vuelan trinos
desde el mástil muy alto
el más cercano borde del azul,
vacila, lo borda por segundos,
recompone una malla,
tensa un vacío, mira con ojo exacto
las quietas margaritas
y vuelve, en un vuelo gracioso,
vigía sin paz,
a la misma, persistente atalaya
donde lo descubrí.
No le importa, sensato,
lo pasajero, lo que abajo pasa,
gente sin ton ni son,
sin música,
agobiada de urgencias.
Él canta por su especie
como no lo hace el hombre.

Mockingbird and Daisies

Here again the mockingbird,
the nightingale of day,
acrobat through silvery winds.
It's March again,
for him pure joy, and he dances
and in that impulse trills fly out
from the lofty flag pole
to the closest edge of blue,
wavering, he embroiders it for seconds,
mends a screen,
tautens a void, eyes with precision
the unmoving daisies
and returns, with a charming swoop,
lookout without peace,
to the same, persistent watchtower
where I discovered him.
Sensibly, he doesn't care
about the temporal, what passes below,
people without rhyme or reason,
without music,
burdened with urgencies.
He sings for his species
as mankind never does.

Gratitudes del verano

En el verano:
viento de la esquina,
verde sobreviviente en la sequía,
tenue, obstinada nube que aparece
y cruza sola el cielo imperturbable,
agasajo de la sombra del árbol,
vaso de agua al regreso: muchas gracias.

Rapado, el pasto tiene olores
a pequeño cadáver indeciso,
otra culpa del verano profundo.
Desolada de ferocísimo sol,
esta pared lo escupe. Sólo faltan
tristezas de pájaros agónicos
para mojar el borde de un pañuelo.

A ti, alfabeto,
gracias te sean dadas,
por acudirme, pese a esta miseria:
musitas y aminoras con memorias
de milagrosas y narradas lluvias,
de mares y manzanas, tanto agobio,
que olvido este calor y que aún lo escribo.

Summer Gratitude

In the summer:
gust of wind on the corner,
green survivor in the drought,
tenuous, obstinate cloud that appears
and crosses the steely sky alone,
gift of the tree's shade,
glass of water upon return: many thanks.

Close-cropped, the grass smells
like a small, indecisive cadaver,
with deep summer to blame again.
Devastated by sun's ferocity,
this wall spits it out. Only sorrows
of moribund birds are missing
to soak the handkerchief's edge.

To you, alphabet,
thanks be given to you,
for succoring me, despite this misery:
you murmur and diminish with memories
of miraculous rains recounted,
of seas and apples, this oppressiveness,
so that I can forget this heat and still write it.

Mi homenaje

Mi homenaje
al que plantó cada árbol
sin pensar, para siempre.
O acaso imaginando al desunido
que un día lo convoca,
lo celebra.

A lo que no obstante el mediodía,
se da en glorioso atardecer.
A todo lo que ocurre
sin ser más que eso: algo.
Al conductor del ómnibus,
cumplido, sonriente,
que levanta una tarde
con su simple saludo.
Al pájaro que pía.
A quien en su país desvencijado
ose decir su parecer riesgoso.
Al que en el valle
recuerda que hay montañas
y en una gota de agua,
olvidando la niebla,
tiembla ante la sequía
y el desierto ofrecido.
Al banco cuya húmeda madera
me acoge y me refresca,
mientras el tormentoso verano
no da tregua.
Al hueco que busca
colmarse pese al vértigo

My Tribute

My tribute
to the one who planted every tree
without thinking: for forever.
Or perhaps imagining the one disunited
who will one day invoke him
in celebration.

To that which, despite midday,
comes to pass in the glory of sunset.
To everything that happens
while being no more than that: something.
To the bus driver,
courteous, smiling,
who uplifts an afternoon
with his simple greeting.
To the bird that cheeps.
To whomever in a rickety country
dares to voice a risky opinion.
To the one in the valley
who remembers there are mountains
and in one drop of water,
forgetting the fog,
trembles before drought
and the desert it promises.
To the bench whose damp wood
welcomes and refreshes me,
while the stormy summer
gives no respite.
To the void that seeks
to brim over despite the vertigo

y a la gaita que llama a soledades
desde un acantilado.
Al que se acuerda de mí.
Al que me olvida.

Libro

Aunque nadie te busque ya, te busco.
Una frase fugaz y cobro glorias
de ayer para los días taciturnos,
en lengua de imprevistas profusiones.

Lengua que usa de un viento peregrino
para volar sobre quietudes muertas.
Viene de imaginaria estación dulce;
va hacia un inexorable tiempo solo.

Don que se ofrece entre glosadas voces,
para tantos equívoco, se obstina
en hundirse, honda raíz de palma,
convicto de entenderse con los pocos.

and to the bagpipes that hail solitude
from the cliff's edge.
To the one who remembers me.
To the one who forgets.

Book

Though no one seeks you now, I seek you.
A fleeting phrase and I recover glories
past for taciturn tomorrows
in a language of unheralded profusion.

Language that harnesses the errant wind
to soar above the dead stillness.
It hails from a sweet season of fancy;
it moves toward the inexorable solitude of time.

This gift bestowed between voices glossed
and misconstrued by many, obstinately stays
submerged, the palm tree's deepest root,
convicted of communing with the few.

Nombre en el viento

Busca ese nombre y se le esconde
en el orden del diccionario.
Olió la hoja y su recuerdo,
saltó la palabra a sus labios
y las letras danzaron,
unidas por un instante
antes de volver a ser libres.
El misterio escapó vuelto aire
en la increíble fragilidad del tiempo,
hacia aquel patio,
el sitio verde de la infancia,
un instante en la historia
de una casa
y ésta en la de un país.
Un coágulo agreste
cuyos cimientos pocos ya
conocen, aman.

Name in the Wind

She seeks that name and it eludes her
in the order of the dictionary.
She nosed the page and her memory,
the word jumped to her lips,
and the letters danced,
united for an instant
before being freed again.
The mystery escaped as air
in the incredible fragility of time,
toward that courtyard,
the green place of childhood,
an instant in the history
of a house
and this in the history of a country.
A wild coagulation
whose foundations few now
know, love.

Círculo muy vicioso

A mí misma me ofrezco
aprender día a día en el mundo,
luego al mundo le ofrezco
día a día olvidarlo,
para yo no ser menos.

Porque el riesgo
de ser menos se corre
si no se olvida mucho
de lo algo aprendido
y además entendido
y tenazmente atroz.
Tras lo vertiginoso,
recordar el olvido
abre la calma.
Y basta.

A Very Vicious Circle

I offer myself
to learn day by day in the world,
then I offer the world
to forget it day by day,
so that I am no less.

Because you run
the risk of being less
by not forgetting much
of the little that's learned
and also understood
and tenaciously vile.
After this vertigo,
remembering to forget
opens stillness.
And is enough.

Programa

1

Recuerda, clara y lentamente, el agua.
Escucha al pájaro:
                    ¿canta apenas su miedo
o demuestra esperanza?

Llega a la rosa y piensa en ella.

No te preocupe el hombre.
Él se basta:
            a solas
prepara su cuchillo.

2

Mira, sin olvidar fatalidades,
la creciente, mas disminuida especie.
Ánclate en lo que tantos desdeñan,
discreta ignora lo que tantos buscan,
para sí recibir, ya sin enfado,
tu bandera sin viento, que desciende.

3

Abre los ojos
a cada parcela de mundo,
brotes de sauce o rostro apático.
Una vez más quedarás deslumbrada
o buscarás tus culpas en el aire:

todavía eres presa de la vida.

Program

1

Remember, clearly and slowly, water.
Listen to the bird:
                                does it sing only fear
or is hope revealed?

Reach the rose and ponder it.

Don't worry about man.
He's enough unto himself:
                                alone
he readies his knife.

2

Observe, not overlooking misfortunes,
the growing but diminished species.
Cling to what so many disdain,
discreetly ignore what they seek,
so you may receive, now without vexation,
your windless flag, which lowers.

3

Open your eyes
to each plot of earth,
shoots of willow or a listless face.
Once again, you'll be awestruck
or you'll seek your offenses in the air:

you're still prisoner to life.

Mar de duda

Mirar la fruta, el mar con ojos de desierto,
la sinrazón con ojos de sordera,
el pasado como al volcán sus estrías de lava
y del futuro su suspensión de infancia,

cuando una sabiduría asombrada
adelantaba penas
y la única indiscutida certeza de la vida
sería osar la luz:

que alguna vez habría
paz en la red,
no un mar de duda.

Andén

Si has visto los círculos lentos
e insistidos del gavilán,
teme la constancia
del gavilán humano
en la bajada precisa y enemiga,
confía en unos pocos seres
—nada más dulce.
Borra los otros.
Partir de modo lento
te permite abrigarte,
en el repaso de la dicha,
del miedo no pensado,
ambos en conciliación ritual.
Ama por ósmosis,
quietísima.

Sea of Doubt

To see the fruit, the sea with desert eyes,
unreason with deaf eyes,
the past as a volcano seen by its lava striations,
and the future's infancy in abeyance,

when an astonished wisdom
hastened sorrows
and the only incontestable certainty in life
is the audacity of light:

if only once there'd be
peace in the net,
not a sea of doubt.

Platform

If you've seen the hawk's
slow, insistent circles,
fear the resolve
of the human hawk
in its precise and hostile swoop,
trust only a few beings
—nothing sweeter.
Erase the rest.
Departing slowly
lets you take shelter
in the retrospection of joy
and unthought-of fear,
both in ritual conciliation.
Love by osmosis,
perfectly still.

Fortuna

Por años, disfrutar del error
y de su enmienda,
haber podido hablar, caminar libre,
no existir mutilada,
no entrar o sí en iglesias,
leer, oír la música querida,
ser en la noche un ser como en el día.

No ser casada en un negocio,
medida en cabras,
sufrir gobierno de parientes
o legal lapidación.
No desfilar ya nunca
y no admitir palabras
que pongan en la sangre
limaduras de hierro.
Descubrir por ti misma
otro ser no previsto
en el puente de la mirada.

Ser humano y mujer, ni más ni menos.

Fortune

For years, to relish errors
and their amends,
to be able to speak, walk freely,
not endure mutilation,
to not enter churches, or enter,
to read, listen to beloved music,
by night be a being as well as by day.

To not be married off in a transaction,
valued in goats,
to not suffer the dominion of relatives
or legal lapidation.
To not parade ever again
or allow words
that inject iron filings
in your blood.
To discover for yourself
another unforeseen being
on the bridge formed by a gaze.

To be human and woman, no more no less.

Nuevas certezas

Poesía
no complace a la historia,
no cuenta cuentos,
no dialoga
con más palabras
que paciencia el que escucha.
No es caricato ni cariátide.
No se produjo nunca.
Muere, en aire indelicado,
cremastícamente organizada.

¿Proyecto de algún hijo
que corre tras un padre
cuya voz lo amamante?
¿El tren de alguien con prisa?
Mejor puerto desierto,
andén abandonado.

Clausura

De todas partes los hermanos se van:
Octavio un día, Tito al tiempo
y acá Laura y Amalia.
A otros los muertos vivos los borraron.
La franja opaca tiembla al extenderse
en borroso boceto
y pasa la golondrina solitaria
y la tapa del cielo se ha amustiado
y yo voy caminando
de pronto hacia el asombro en que no creo.

New Certainties

Poetry
doesn't cater to history,
it doesn't tell tales,
nor converse
with more words
than the listener has patience for.
It's not caricature nor caryatid.
It was never produced.
It dies, in the indelicate air,
chrematistically organized.

The project of a child
running after his father
whose voice nurses him?
The train of someone in a hurry?
Better: a deserted port,
an abandoned platform.

Closure

From every direction, bretheren depart:
Octavio one day, Tito in time,
and here, Laura and Amalia.
The living dead erased the others.
The opaque border trembles while spreading
in a hazy outline,
and the solitary swallow passes
and the cover to the sky has withered
and I go walking
one day toward the wonder I don't believe in.

Grajo muerto

Tiene un nombre la muerte
pero el amor de nadie.
Nada averigua y sin mitologías
ni piedad, por todas partes muerde.
También la tiene así enseñada,
en lo que puede, el hombre.

Encuentro al grajo negriazul
—en cada pluma intacta
el minucioso tornasol—
cerrados los ojos siempre atentos
y blando el cuello, enhiesto
en la provocación del amor,
su cola, ese timón al viento,
nunca más singular.
Con admirarlo y condolerme
le alzo su etérea tumba
y doy un paso, también yo,
hacia el campo con nombre,
sin palabras, sin resplandor de nadie.

Dead Grackle

Death has a name
but no one's love.
Uncovering nothing, with no mercy
or mythologies, it bites near and far.
Man, too, has trained it that way,
as best he can.

I find the bluish-black grackle
—in each intact feather
a meticulous iridescence—
his ever-attentive eyes closed
and neck soft, once upright
in the provocation of love,
his tail, that wind rudder,
never more singular.
With admiration and grief,
I raise his ethereal grave
and take a step, myself,
toward that field with a name,
with no words or anyone's radiance.

Calesita

El carrusel, el tiovivo, el cómo
se llamaba, la calesita, llama
que me ofrecía un ciervo, una calesa,
un cisne y un caballo encabritado,
el prodigio que giraba tan quieto,
que tan quieto trotaba por un aire
con organillo y campanillas, aire
que no movía la cola del caballo
dorado y blanco, pero de peligro,
peligro de caerme en pleno vuelo,
de caerme y quedar así olvidada
del padre, de bajar en otro punto
del punto de subida y verme sola,
sin nubes, sin ya viento en el pelo,
perdida sin el miedo delicioso
de volar con las manos aferradas
a crines que me sueltan y yo arcilla
que en el horno del aire recupera
su forma quieta, forma del principio,
de ser sola y sin alas.

Merry-Go-Round

The carousel, the roundabout, the what-
do-you-call-it, the merry-go-round, it called
to me, a candle flame, with a stag, a coach,
a swan and a horse, a rearing horse,
a marvel that circled around so still,
so still it trotted up through the air
with organ pipes and little bells, the air
not moving the tail of the horse
so golden and white, but dangerous,
the danger of falling off in midflight,
of falling and being forgotten
by father, of getting off elsewhere
than where I got on, all at once alone,
without clouds or wind now in my hair,
just lost without the delectable fear
of flying with both hands clutched
to the mane that frees me, and I am clay
in the kiln of air that slowly recovers
its stillness of form, the form of beginnings,
of being alone without wings.

En el portal oscuro

La tú misma con la que te rozaste,
la que no podrá llegar a ser
en lo poco que queda,
la que quiso haber sido
y una suma de instantes astillados
de la vida apartaron
de los sin duda sueños:
¿cuál cierta entre lo incierto?
Ya no claves: candores
y epidermis más o menos expuesta.
Y un silencio de gruta
bajo el bosque estridente.
Soñabas en el claro embrujado
en el centro de lo enredado oscuro,
en las señas intactas y las guías
y el portal todo luz.
Ése por donde se volvía
al comienzo,
a la voz sin fractura.
A la feliz, irracional certeza.

In the Dark Entryway

The you that you brushed against,
the woman who'll never come to be
in the little that is left,
the one who wanted to have been
but a sum of life's
shattered moments separated
from what doubtless were dreams:
which you was true among uncertainty?
No more secret keys: candor
and a mostly exposed epidermis.
And a cavern's silence
beneath the strident forest.
You dreamed in the enchanted clearing
at the heart of the dark tangle,
in intact signs and guides,
and an entryway of light.
The one that returned
to the beginning,
to the unfractured voice.
To happy, irrational certainty.

Nuevas obligaciones

Tendré que hacer una nevada montaña
de este montón de harina,

un bosque de estas tres enfiladas encinas
que miro y están solas,

una cascada del chorro de agua fría
que mi mano intercepta

y de la concesión, un géiser.

Desconectada, como erizo sin su cueva entre el pasto,
tendré que prevenirme de tanta ímproba realidad,

alta en el árbol del malestar,
como mono que va perdiendo su selva.

En el aire

Un jardín de geranios y su aire.
Junto a su cerca dejo que paste
el buey que pesa sobre mi lengua
y digo: Aquí te quedas, come
en verde dehesa, pero terrena,
y canta, luego, si puedes,
si nadie escucha,
lo que queda por no decir.

New Obligations

I'll have to make a snow-covered mountain
from this mound of flour,

a forest from these three live oaks in a row
that I see and are alone,

a cascade from this jet of cold water
that my hand intercepts

and from concession, a geyser.

Disconnected, like a hedgehog without its burrow in the grass,
I'll have to prepare for unscrupulous reality,

high in the tree of discontent,
like a monkey that is losing its jungle.

In the Air

A garden of geraniums and its air.
Close to the fence I let graze
the ox that weighs on my tongue
and say: Stay right here, eat
of this green but earthly pasture,
and sing, then, if you can,
if no one's listening,
all that remains to be unsaid.

Acaso explicación

Alguien se va para no irse,
para quedar encapsulado
en un pasado imaginario,
páramo del nunca olvidar.

Puede entender bajo otro cielo
cómo un pájaro dice gracias,
la lenta fuerza del pabilo
y el regresar a la constancia.

Disuelto, extinto, lo mentido
una vía del mal se vuelve,
por donde hombres como troncos,
rinden sus sueños, sólo flotan.

Aun muertos, muchos son atasco,
dioses con dosis de veneno.
Pero se guarda en un reflejo
un pequeño sol. Siempreviva.

Possible Explanation

Someone leaves to not go away,
to stay encapsulated
in an imaginary past,
the wasteland of memory.

Under a different sky one understands
how a bird gives thanks,
the slow strength of a wick
and the return to constancy.

Dissolved, extinct, the lies
become a passage of evil
where men, like tree trunks,
surrender their dreams, only float.

Even dead, many are obstructions,
deities with doses of venom.
But a reflection safekeeps
a small sun within. Everlasting.

Llamada vida

Ponerse al margen
asistir a un pan
cantar un himno

menoscabarse en vano
abrogar voluntades
refrendar cataclismos

acompañar la soledad
no negarse a las quimeras
remansarse en el tornado

ir de lo ceñido a lo vasto
desde lo opaco a la centella
de comisión al sueño libre

ofrecerse a lo parco del día
si morir una hora tras otra
volver a comenzar cada noche

volar de lo distinto a lo idéntico
admirar miradores y sótanos
infligirse penarse concernirse

estar en busca de alma diferida
preparar un milagro entre la sombra
y llamar vida a lo que sabe a muerte.

So-Called Life

To stand at the margin
tend to a loaf of bread
sing a hymn

shrink oneself in vain
abrogate volition
endorse cataclysms

accompany solitude
not refuse chimeras
slow down inside a tornado

go from restricted to vast
from opacity to a spark
from tasks to liberated dreams

give oneself to the meagerness of day
if dying hour upon hour
begin again each night

fly from the distinct to the identical
admire overlooks and undergrounds
inflict mourn be concerned

be on watch for a deferred soul
prepare a miracle in the shadow
and call this life when it tastes of death.

Vórtice

La hoja en blanco
atrae como la tragedia,
traspasa como la precisión,
traga como el pantano,
te traduce como lo hace la trivialidad,
te engaña como sólo tú mismo puedes hacerlo.
Atrapa con la dominación del delirio,
encierra todo el dolor
o la ya tan difícil exaltación.
Sobre todo cumple pretorianamente
tu encomienda: te veda
la justicia por propia pluma.

Cultura del palimpsesto

Todo aquí es palimpsesto,
pasión del palimpsesto:

a la deriva,
              borrar lo poco hecho,
empezar de la nada,
afirmar la deriva,
mirarse entre la nada acrecentada,
velar lo venenoso,
matar lo saludable,
escribir delirantes historias para náufragos.

Cuidado:
no se pierde sin castigo el pasado,
no se pisa en el aire.

Vortex

The blank page
attracts like tragedy,
pierces with precision,
swallows like a swamp,
it translates you as triviality,
it deceives you as only you yourself do.
It lays traps with the power of delirium,
enclosing all pain
or the already so arduous exaltation.
Above all, it fulfills praetorian-wise
your assignment: denying you
justice by your own pen.

A Culture of Palimpsest

Everything here is palimpsest,
a passion for palimpsest:

adrift,
        erase the little achieved,
start from nothing,
affirm the drifting,
watch oneself in the growing nothing,
veil the venomous,
kill the salubrious,
write delirious stories for the shipwrecked.

Careful:
the past is not lost without punishment,
you cannot walk on air.

Paréntesis, casa frágil

Cuando la cerrazón arrecie
abre paréntesis, signo tibio,
casa frágil
que no tiene más techo
que el cielo imaginado
(aunque sea adusto, ácido, aciago,
si es otro quien lo abre),

piensa dos manos
que protejan tu rostro,
de veras miren dentro de ti,
agrupen sol contra el invierno,
sol y solvencia humana.

Aunque debas cruzar
bosques de tiempo,
pisar tantas hojas secas
en el suelo de la memoria,
cuidar no ser tragado
por zanjas de sorpresiva erosión,
búscate en el paréntesis,
como en palabras para siempre calladas.

Parentheses, Fragile Shelter

When storm clouds thicken
open parentheses, tepid sign,
fragile shelter
with no roof beyond
the imagined sky
(though it may be austere, acerbic, adverse,
if it's someone else who opens them),

imagine two hands
protecting your face,
truly seeing within you,
gathering sun for the winter,
sun and human solvency.

Even if you must cross
forests of time,
trample countless dry leaves
on the ground of memory,
and take care not to be swallowed
by trenches of startling erosion,
seek yourself in parentheses,
as in words forever unspoken.

Traducir

Alguien desborda,
al centro de la noche.
Ante un orden de palabras ajenas,
rebelde sometido,
ofrece el canto de toda su memoria,
las reviste de nueva piel
y con amor
las duerme en nueva lengua.

Apagada la luz,
el viento se pregona entre los árboles
y junto a la ventana hay frío
y la certeza de que todo paisaje
adentro se interrumpe
como frase que alcanza la madriguera
del terrible sentido.
No hay dispuesto
en el yermo
un benévolo guía.

Los pasos son a ciegas,
el cielo sin estrellas.
Y el pensamiento anticipa las fieras.

To Translate

Someone overflows
at the center of the night.
Facing the order of another's words,
subjugated rebel,
she offers the song of her whole memory,
she sheathes them in new skin
and lovingly
puts them to sleep in a new tongue.

                              Lights off,
the wind trumpets in the trees
and there's a chill close to the window
and the certainty that every landscape
is disrupted within
like a sentence that reaches the lair
of formidable meaning.
                          There is no
benevolent guide
              waiting in the wasteland.

Steps are taken blindly,
starless the sky.
And thought anticipates wild beasts.

Sumas

caballo y caballero son ya dos animales
—J. D. García Bacca

Uno más uno, decimos. Y pensamos:
una manzana más una manzana,
un vaso más un vaso,
siempre cosas iguales.

Qué cambio cuando
uno más uno sea un puritano
más un gamelán,
un jazmín más un árabe,
una monja y un acantilado,
un canto y una máscara,
otra vez una guarnición y una doncella,
la esperanza de alguien
más el sueño de otro.

Sums

horse and horseman are already two animals
—J. D. García Bacca

One plus one, we say. And think:
one apple plus one apple,
one glass plus one glass,
always equal things.

What a difference when
one plus one is a Puritan
plus a gamelan,
a jasmine plus an Arab,
a nun and an escarpment,
a song and a mask,
once again a garrison and a maiden,
the hope of someone
plus the dream of another.

Gotas

¿Se hieren y se funden?
Acaban de dejar de ser la lluvia.
Traviesas en recreo,
gatitos de un reino transparente,
corren libres por vidrios y barandas,
umbrales de su limbo,
se siguen, se persiguen,
quizá van, de soledad a bodas,
a fundirse y amarse.
Trasueñan otra muerte.

Otoño

Otoño, perro
de cariñosa pata impertinente,
mueve las hojas de los libros.
Reclama que se atienda
las fascinantes suyas,
que en vano pasan del verde
al oro al rojo al púrpura.

Como en la distracción,
la palabra precisa
que pierdes para siempre.

Droplets

Do they rend apart and meld together?
They've just stopped being the rain.
Mischievous at play,
kittens from a transparent realm,
they run freely down windowpanes and railings,
thresholds of their limbo,
racing each other, chasing each other,
perhaps from solitude to nuptials,
to meld together and love each other.
They dream another death.

Autumn

Autumn, dog
with affectionate, impertinent paws,
rustles the leaves of the books.
He demands that you pay attention
to those fetching ones that are his,
that futilely turn from green
to gold to red to purple.

As if in distraction,
the precise word
escapes you forever.

Patrimonio

Sólo tendremos lo que hayamos dado.
¿Y qué con lo ofrecido y no aceptado,
qué con aquello que el desdén reduce
a vana voz, sin más,
ardiente ántrax que crece,
desatendido, adentro?

La villanía del tiempo,
el hábito sinuoso
del tolerar paciente,
difiere frágiles derechos,
ofrece minas, socavones, grutas:
oscuridad apenas para apartar
        vagos errores.

El clamor, letra a letra,
del discurso agorero
no disipa ninguna duda;
hace mucho que sabes:
        ninguna duda te protege.

Patrimony

We will only have what we have given.
And what about things offered and not accepted,
all that disdain reduces
to vain voices, without warning,
ardent anthrax that grows
in neglect within?

The villainy of time,
the sinuous habit
of patient tolerance,
defers frangible rights,
offers mines, sinkholes, grottos:
just enough darkness to separate
      indistinct errors.

Letter upon letter, the clamor
of the ominous oration
dissipates no doubt;
you've known for so long:
      no doubt can protect you.

Árboles

¿Es la encina de Orlando o son éstas de Austin?
¿Es el ombú de Hudson o aquél junto al que el auto
arrastró de la vida a Julio-casi-hermano?
¿El baniano de Paz, que era el de Sakuntala?
¿Sauces de Garcilaso?, ¿el que planté yo misma?
¿Álamos del amor, o aquel del que en invierno
caían a mis pies pájaros casi muertos?
¿Las higueras constantes, entre polvo y jardines?
¿Ese eje en el tropismo de lunas infinitas,
el eucalipto pálido, de plumón perfumado?
¿Los de flor color lacre bajo soles de incendio?
¿Abedul que creí negro, por ébano/abenuz,
hasta que toqué blanca su corteza anillada?
¿El árbol esencial que imaginaba Goethe?
¿O aquel con cuya sombra perdí el mundo
que era rumor de voces amistosas
y veo pasar un río que sí es el mismo siempre,
en tanto que lo miro y ya no soy la misma?

Trees

Is this Orlando's oak or are these oaks from Austin?
Is this Hudson's ombú or the one beside the car
that dragged Julio-my-almost-brother from life?
Paz's banyan tree, that was also Shakuntala's?
The willows of Garcilaso? The one that I myself planted?
Poplars of love, or that one in winter
from which half-dead birds fell at my feet?
Trusty figs, among the dust and gardens?
That axis in the tropism of infinite moons,
a pale eucalyptus of perfumed down?
Those with lacquer-red flowers under fiery suns?
The birch/abedul I imagined black, for the ebony/abenuz,
until I touched its white, ringed bark?
The essential tree of Goethe's imagination?
Or the one in whose shade I lost the world
that was itself a murmur of friendly voices
and I see a river flow that is the same always,
whereas I watch it and am no longer the same?

Anunciación

Viene el ángel de raso, replegadas las alas,
hacia el rincón de la terraza donde,
al pie de la columna,
leía la virgen el libro que ahora olvida.
Un gozque, junto a ella,
alza una pata inquieta, mientras,
contra el crepúsculo,
del dedo admonitorio del ángel
diríase que un hilo parte
y doblega una mano dócil
sobre el pecho asustado.
Los colores
son los que acostumbra el Veronese:
borra de vino el talar de María,
oscuro azul su manto.
El cielo en el crepúsculo progresa
del intenso celeste a los jirones rosa
que anuncian para mañana,
acaso, la tormenta.
Pero ya cuaja un leve
velo gris sobre las cosas
que ignoran
cómo se leerá su destino.

Todo sucede a una distancia abismal
de este mundo,
que aún se imagina libre
de la Bestia y del Límite.

Annunciation

The angel in satin comes, wings folded,
toward the corner of the terrace where,
at the foot of the column,
the virgin was reading a book now forgotten.
A lap dog by her side
raises a nervous paw while,
against the twilight,
from the angel's admonishing finger
a thread seems to extend,
folding her docile hand
against her startled breast.
The colors
are Veronese's usual ones:
Mary's robe, the color of grape skins,
dark blue, her cloak.
The sky at dusk progresses
from deep azure to wisps of pink
that foretell tomorrow's
possible storm.
But already a light
gray veil settles over things
that ignore
how their destiny will be read.

Everything occurs at an abysmal distance
from this world
that still imagines itself free
from the Beast and the Limit.

La gloria de Filitis

Nada labró Filitis, pastor egipcio.
Fue pobre.
No intuyó nueva barca
de líneas más seguras y bellas.
No imaginó jardines
ni un trazo ni una música,
no dejó nada escrito,
no movió una figura del sagrado perfil.

Sólo llevó sus bestias a pacer
al pie de las colinas
donde Quefrén y Queops,
los execrables reyes,
durante medio siglo
levantaron sus tumbas
sobre hombros de pueblos agotados.

Éstos, abominándolos,
no quisieron nombrarlos.
Justicieros decían
para hablar de esos sitios:
—Allí,
donde las pirámides de Filitis.

The Glory of Philitis

Philitis, Egyptian shepherd, built nothing.
He was poor.
He didn't dream up a new boat
with safer and more beautiful lines.
He didn't envisage gardens
or brushstrokes or songs,
he left nothing in writing,
he changed nothing of the profile's sacred form.

He only took his beasts to graze
at the foot of the hills
where Chephren and Cheops,
execrable kings,
for half a century
erected their tombs
on the shoulders of exhausted peoples.

These, out of hate,
refused to utter those two names.
With righteousness they'd say
when speaking of those sites:
"There,
by the pyramids of Philitis."

Estornino

Como si el estornino
no tuviese otra cosa para el asombro
que su nombre.
¿Pero en quién sino en él
obra el dorado?
Lo primero es su pico,
próximo a todo.
¿Y esas chispas de oro de sus plumas?
Vestido así igual trajina
entre los pastos de la tierra.
Va como un caballero medieval,
pronto para el torneo o el asalto
o el polvo del camino
en sus ropas de noble vagamundos.
Experiente y arisco,
con él no cabe diálogo ni ofrenda.
Quizás el ojo de Ahura Mazda
contemplando en Persépolis
el raso oscuro de sus galas,
lo dejó tachonado de fulgores
y él no lo ignore.

Starling

As if the starling
left nothing to wonder
but his name.
For in whom but him
is the auric at work?
First it's his beak,
in proximity to everything.
And those flecks of gold in his feathers?
Even dressed this way he bustles
about the grasses of the earth.
Like a medieval knight,
he's ready for a tournament or a siege
or the dust from the road
in his clothes of a noble vagabond.
Experienced and aloof, with him
there's no room for dialogue or oblation.
Perhaps the eye of Ahura Mazda
contemplating in Persepolis
the dark satin of his regalia
left him spangled with brilliance
and of that he is not unaware.

Caracol

El caracol va con apuro
aunque la gente no lo crea
y piense que sólo pasea
en busca de sol por el muro.

Al contrario, quien en lo oscuro
sus calcáreas burbujas vea,
sepa: ni duerme ni procrea.
Deseoso de mejor futuro,

ha resuelto cambiar de casa.
Y no codicia un rascacielo
con harto hierro y argamasa,

y sí donde el hornero anida.
Pronto lo verán por el hielo
buscando un iglú a su medida.

Snail

The snail moves with expedition
though people don't believe it
and think he only transits
the wall in search of warm sun.

On the contrary, if you happen on
his chalky bubbles in the umbra,
know: he neither mates nor slumbers.
Desiring better days to come,

he's resolved to swap his home.
It's not a skyscraper he eyes
with iron and mortar overblown

but the nest where the ovenbird abides.
Soon you'll find him crossing ice
in search of an igloo just his size.

Serie del sinsonte

... and if men should not hear them men are old.
—E. E. Cummings

1

Iridiscente en lo más alto de su canto
entre dos luces libre celebra, labra
un elíseo de música en un árbol,
el pájaro burlón, el sinsonte de marzo.

Por la noche sumó nuestros silencios,
los halló opacos, sin centella;
entonces, como un delfín del aire,
hace su prestidigitación de amanecida.

Va hacia arriba con dicha de ráfaga,
sólo afín a su vértigo propio,
pero regresa siempre a lo discreto,
al negro, al blanco, al gris en que se esconde.

Pone su voz corona donde elige
cima para entregarse a calma o viento,
virazón de delicia en el desierto
del total desarraigo y desaliento.

Él delira sensato en su fragmento.
Tan perfecto este diálogo, este lento
juego de acompañarse y no entenderse
a solas cada uno con su sueño.

2

Canta eterno el sinsonte en el árbol
y es rocío que el sueño refresca,

The Mockingbird Series

... and if men should not hear them men are old.
—E. E. Cummings

1

Iridescent at the height of his song,
free between two lights to celebrate, create
an Elysium of music in a tree,
the mimicking mockingbird of March.

By night he made sums of our silences,
he found them opaque, without spark;
since then, like an aerial dolphin,
he performs his conjuring at dawn.

He soars up with the joy of a windburst,
akin only to his own vertigo,
but he always returns to discretion,
to black, white, gray shades where he hides.

His voice crowns the peak he picks
to surrender himself to the calm or wind,
delectable sea breeze in a desert
of complete disseverance and dismay.

Sound of mind, he raves in his fragment.
So perfect this dialogue, this slow
game of accompaniment and dissonance
each one by himself with his dream.

2

The mockingbird sings eternal in the tree
and is dew that refreshes dreams,

ola que espuma la punta lejana,
irreversible Iguazú que imagino;

canta el pájaro y cruzamos el vado
¿no se escucha la losa, la túnica,
una risa que aplaza relojes,
un relato que rueda en los siglos?

Canta el pájaro aquí y entreabre
la cerrada, distante ventana
a un silencio que puede ser música
pero nunca sinsonte. ¿Calandria?

3
El largo día es su escenario.
Preciso pasa, precipita cristales,
violas y flautas, triángulos y burla.

Anuncia, ruega, ofrece y nunca queda corto
y hace llover la deliciosa sombra
que al mediodía siempre se le olvida.

Apaga pálidas sirenas
para ofrecer *Gato maltés azul*
a los que nada ven y nada escuchan.

A los hastiados dice que soñemos,
en el espacio de nuestra ceguera,
otro lugar, otro tiempo pasado.

a wave that foams the distant point,
irreversible Iguazú of my imagination;

the bird sings and we cross the ford.
Can't you hear the gravestone, the tunic,
a laughter that sets clocks back,
a tale tumbling through centuries?

The bird sings here, cracking open
the closed, distant window
to a silence that could be music
but never mockingbird: Calandra lark?

3
The long day is his stage.
Precise, he passes, precipitating crystals,
violas and flutes, triangles and mockery.

He announces, begs, offers, and never falls short,
making delicious shadows rain down
that he always forgets by noon.

He extinguishes pale sirens
and offers Un gatto nel blu
to those who see nothing and hear nothing.

To the world-weary, he tells us to dream,
in the space of our blindness,
a different place, a different time gone by.

4
Dice el sinsonte a cada nota:
jilguero, petirrojo, clarín, mirlo
y para que no olvide aquel perfecto
blanco sobre lo blanco de la espuma,
hace un silencio donde vuela,
sol y sal solos, la gaviota.

Montevideo

Límpida fresca y eléctrica
era la luz y el cielo leve
como el final de una paciencia.
Lejanísimos nubes, nombres,
cercana a la vez una salva
de golondrinas por el aire
pero en honor de nada o nadie.

¿Cómo llegamos a este vano
marco de marzo hacia el vacío?
La seducción, no del abismo:
de poza quieta y sus insectos.
Puede lo bello ser un hueco:
las desoladas quemazones
sobre una tierra distraída
de lo que un día hubiera sido.

4
The mockingbird says with each note:
goldfinch, robin, thrush, blackbird,
and so as not to forget that perfect
white on the whiteness of foam,
he creates a silence wherever flies,
in a solo of sun and salt, the seagull.

Montevideo

Limpid fresh and electric
was the light and the sky gentle,
like the end of a patience.
Faraway clouds, names,
while nearby, a salvo
of swallows in the air
but in honor of nothing and no one.

How did we come to this vain
frame of March near the void?
The seduction, not of the abyss:
of a quiet pool and its insects.
Beauty can be a hollow:
the devastated burnings
over a land distracted
from what once could have been.

Translator's note: Opening lines in italics are from Dino Campana's poem "Viaggio a Montevideo" ("Journey to Montevideo").

Soltar el mirlo

Hablaremos, árboles claros,
después que el viento se haya ido.

    *

Arde este tajamar de inundaciones graves.
El gamonal de arriba no lo impide.

    *

Aun el árbol engaña.
Sólo la música dice un paraíso.

    *

El fuego quemó sinuoso el campo.
Hoy su cicatriz es la lengua más verde.

    *

Andar lo más posible sobre trébol.
Tropezar prueba la cercanía del cielo.

    *

Leuda la luz sobre un caballo blanco.
Los tersos benteveos se dibujan cantando.

Set the Blackbird Free

We will talk, sunlit trees,
after the wind has passed.

       *

This breakwater of grievous inundations burns.
The cacique up above doesn't impede it.

       *

Even the tree is deceptive.
Only music speaks paradise.

       *

Sinuous, the fire burned the field.
Today its scar is the greenest tongue.

       *

Walk the most you can on clover.
Stumbling proves the nearness of the sky.

       *

Light leavens over a white horse.
The glossy kiskadees manifest by singing.

Paloma

Posada la paloma
en la pared blanquísima
blanca es y reverbera,
es de veras,
                es verbo,
nos venga.
Blanca posada pide,
pasajera.

De pronto es negra.
                Vuela.

Marzo

Marzo marítimo mana fulgores.
Jugos súbitos entre las copas
brindan por el misterio
de este tiempo vacío de magia
pese a su bando de prodigioso,
prodigante otoño.
Nada, sino los modos del sueño,
habrá cambiado. Nada,
excepto los alivios del olvido.
Condiciones de luz y de desánimo.
Y no hay Madagascar incandescente.

Pigeon

The pigeon perched
on the whitest wall
is white and reverberates,
it veritably is
                    it is verb,
avenging us.
A white shelter, it pleads,
a passenger in passing.

Suddenly it's black.
                    Flight.

March

Maritime March emanates glimmering light.
Sudden sap in the crowns of trees
toasts the mystery
of this time devoid of magic
despite its proclamation of a prodigious,
prodigal fall.
Nothing, save the ways of dreams
will have changed. Nothing,
but oblivion's respite.
Conditions of light and despondency.
And there is no incandescent Madagascar.

Imagen del mundo flotante

Avanza recto el amatista,
                    sin ambages,
da, cruento,
            sobre el amaranto carmesí
y centellea en el sumiso cristal.
Cuesta sobreponerse a este doble poniente.
Esa vidriada imagen que te ciega,
como a veces el mundo,
aquí, donde nada puede durar,
pronto será flamante ruina.
En tanto, multiplica runas
de dramático aviso
que dicen malandanza y danza
de la muerte
y aguardas ver tu reflejo allí,
humo flotante:

          Es amargo ser Tántalo. ¿Vale amar?
          Igual pasas crujía,
          inauguras tus peores augurios.

Mientras llegue la noche,
una vez más cerrada, sigilada,
sigues, válganos Dios,
macerando en ese mismo alcohol
la pupila, el pabilo del alma
que ve los males que la matan.

Image of the Floating World

Amethyst advances straight ahead,
                                    directly,
falls, bloody,
                on crimson amaranth
and shimmers in the submissive pane.
It's hard to overcome this dual sunset.
This vitreous image that blinds you,
as the world sometimes does,
here, where nothing can last,
will soon be brand-new ruins.
For now, runes multiply
with dramatic warnings
foretelling the discordance and dance
of death.
You hope to see your reflection there,
floating smoke:

      It's bitter being Tantalus. Is it worth loving?
      Likewise you are crushed,
         inaugurating your worst augurles.

Until night falls,
once again enclosed, sealed,
you continue, God help us,
steeping in that same alcohol
your pupil, the soul's wick,
that observes the evils that kill it.

Calendario

En enero morimos,
febriles de febrero,
                    frágiles
frente al fatuo fuego frustráneo
de este tiempo.
Nos rodea el vacío
y allí lanzamos nuestro grito
y suena a hueco
                    una hueca caverna como

                    hueca hueca
y no sabremos si no hemos matado
una serpiente
que dormía sin culpa.

Nada
ocupa más lugar de duelo
que el eco de las profecías.
En tanto la esperanza hace túneles y túneles
que cae como esa voz o piedra,
dando voces
en el incomprendido lenguaje
                    de la piedra.

Calendar

In January we die,
febrile for February,
                              fragile
facing the fatuous, frustrating fire
of these times.
The void surrounds us
and we hurl our scream
and it sounds hollow
                              a hollow cavern as if

                              hollow hollow
and we won't know if we haven't killed
a serpent
asleep, without sin.

Nothing
takes more space for grieving
than the echo of prophecies.
Meanwhile hope digs tunnels and tunnels,
collapses like that voice or stone,
thundering
in the unfathomable language
                              of stone.

Clinamen

Y volveremos siempre al sesgo
del clinamen,
al riesgo de apartarse del punto del pasado
donde aún el dardo tiembla,
para recomenzar.

¿De salirse de madre vendrá
el encontrar la madreperla, acaso
la perla sin prisiones?

Sin prisas derivar,
aunque cambie de nombre el distraerse
del paso de los años,
del peso de las mañas ajenas
y de la anulación
de las mañanas.

Claridad, caridad:
volver a aclimatarse
                    en
                       el
                          declive.

Clinamen

And we'll always return to the swerve
of the clinamen,
to the risk of diverging from the point in the past
where the dart still trembles
in order to recommence.

From the overflowing of mother
will the mother-of-pearl be found, perhaps
that pearl without prisons?

Unhurriedly drift,
though the name of distraction
from the passage of the years,
from the pressure of others' mores
and the revocation
of all tomorrows, may change.

Clarity, charity:
acclimate again
                to
                    this
                        declivity.

Exilios

tras tanto acá y allá yendo y viniendo
        —Francisco de Aldana

Están aquí y allá: de paso,
en ningún lado.
Cada horizonte: donde un ascua atrae.
Podrían ir hacia cualquier grieta.
No hay brújula ni voces.

Cruzan desiertos que el bravo sol
o que la helada queman
y campos infinitos sin el límite
que los vuelve reales,
que los haría casi de tierra y pasto.

La mirada se acuesta como un perro,
sin el tierno recurso de mover una cola.
La mirada se acuesta o retrocede,
se pulveriza por el aire,
si nadie la devuelve.
No regresa a la sangre ni alcanza
a quien debiera.

Se disuelve, tan sólo.

Exiles

after so much here and there, coming and going
                                    —Francisco de Aldana

They're here and there: passing through,
nowhere really.
Every horizon: wherever an ember beckons.
They could move toward any crack.
There is no compass, no voices.

They cross deserts burned
by the fiery sun or frost
and infinite fields without the boundaries
that make them real,
that could almost turn them into land and pasture.

A gaze lies down like a dog,
without the sweet recourse of a wagging tail.
A gaze lies down or recedes,
pulverized by the air
if no one returns it.
It can't return to blood or reach
the one it should.

It simply dissolves.

Sicilia

Sicilia, la Trinacria,
desconocida fuente,
de tres cabos:
moriré
sin llevar hasta tu tierra
las memorias oscuras,
un oriol en ormesí pintado,
restos del alma de un familiar combate.
Cosas veladas,
            el caos atisbado
con palabras ajenas
y la colina,
            el oquedal,
la casa de azafrán silenciosa,
arras de la tía abuela Grazia,
cuando,
            bella como la piedra,
la atrapó el claustro
—lejos lloró el hermano—
porque, sola, el demonio acechaba.
Árabes y naranjas
                y canciones
                y ruina.
Llaves para lo que las subterráneas
aguas del alma saben:

el inimaginable
            destino
transgredido.

Sicily

Sicily, the Trinacria,
unknown source
with three capes:
I will die
without taking dark memories
to your land,
an oriole painted on heavy silk,
soul shards from a familial dispute.
Shrouded things,
                chaos glimpsed
in the words of others
and the hill,
          the dense forest,
the silent saffron house,
great-aunt Grazia's wedding coins,
when,
     beautiful as stone,
the convent trapped her
—far away her brother wept—
because the devil lurks when a woman's alone.
Arabs and oranges
             and songs
             and ruin.
Keys for what the underground
waters of the soul know:

that unimaginable
              destiny
transgressed.

A Octavio Paz

Respeto es mirar atrás,
seguir
     en la traviesa del filón
     por más oro,
     por más sazón en lo secreto,
de hilo en ovillo
devanar lo no vano,
lo que ha venido siendo
               forma labrada,
desde trazo,
     partícula inflamada
     o nieve no entendida.

Dichosa como pájaro sobre el césped cortado,
como nube que va hacia su tormenta,
como verdad que se encontró a sí misma,
     palabra
     es patria que vela por sus hijos
desde el génesis,
cada nombre del pájaro,
los nombres de la rosa.

Cruza de norte a sur, profética,
las fronteras de un cuerpo.
Vuelve las certidumbres
que ese cuerpo trasmina
     y las incertidumbres,
en ese pan verbal que a todos
nos ofrece.
     Buceo en lo que fluye
y en lo que aguarda quieto,
palabra Paz reluce.

To Octavio Paz

Respect is looking back,
following
             along the crossbeam of a mine
             for more gold,
             for more ripening in secret,
from a skein of thread,
winding what doesn't dwindle,
what is becoming
                   form wrought
from mere line,
               inflamed particle
          or undeciphered snow.

Happy like a bird in mowed grass,
like a cloud racing toward its storm,
like truth revealed to itself,
        the word
        is the homeland that safeguards its children
since the genesis,
every name of the bird,
the names of the rose.

Prophetic, it crosses the body's borders
from north to south.
It turns certainties
that this body tunnels through,
        as well as uncertainties,
into verbal bread offered
to us all.
        I sink into the flow
and within what waits in stillness
shines the word Paz.

Lo cotidiano

Del cotidiano entreasco
al regreso sabrás:
                    el silencio,
el espacio vaciado
para que el pie vacile.

A la vuelta comienza
                    la muerta
roma disputa yerta
sobre lo traspensado
y lo posmuerto.

Vía brumosa borra
la euforia generosa.
Apela a parir sombra
                    solos,
a seguir en el silencio exacto
que una barca
que navega en los siglos
nos enseña.

Quotidian

From the quotidian inbesqueam
to the return you'll know:

                          silence,

the emptied space
for a foot to falter.

Upon return, the dull

                   dead

inert dispute begins
over the afterthought
and the postmortem.

The murky way erases
euphoria's generosity.
Calls us to birth shadows

                      alone,

to follow in the exact silence
that a boat
that navigates the ages
teaches us.

Translator's note: Opening line in italics is from Oliverio Girondo's poem "Habría" ("There Would Be").

Anafórica

Presente que remite
por más sombra
que luz, hacia el pasado,
sépulcre solide où gît tout ce qui nuit
en cuyas infinitas cavernas
nos espera el recuerdo
de cómo,
      ilusos,
           soñamos el futuro.

Sílaba

Pirarajú, piragua, Piranesi,
soberbios paladines pasajeros,
pájaros prismas apresados
en sílabas sibilas sediciosas
que suman sus enigmas.
Dragantes de un escudo que preserva
arcanos para ciegos.

Anaphoric

This present that refers us
to the past because of
more shadow than light,
the solid sepulcher where all harm lies
in whose infinite caverns
the memory awaits us
of how,
            naively
                    we dreamed the future.

Translator's note: Line in italics from Stéphane Mallarmé's "Toast funèbre" ("Funeral Toast"), translated by Peter Manson.

Syllable

Pirarajú, pirogue, Piranesi,
presumptuous paladins in passing,
passerine prisms apprehended
in seditious sibylline syllables
that equal the sum of their enigmas.
Dragons' heads from a shield preserving
arcana for the blind.

Hamlet (noticias para)

Hoy madre tía y tío padre
mandan en nosotros,
el reino retrocede
a grado de provincia mercenaria.
Huele a milicia en todas las fronteras.

Los ácidos se filtran al oído
no de un triste rey solo,
de adolescentes reyes por millares,
de hombres que reyes fueran
sin esta envenenada rapsodia de mentiras.

Pero ya sabes, príncipe,
que cuando el viento sur sopla en la gente,
las telarañas vuelan
y por oscuro que esté todo en torno
se ven claras "las grullas, los halcones."

Saxífraga

Lección de la saxífraga:
                              florecer
entre piedras,
              atreverse.

Hamlet (News for)

Today aunt-mother and uncle-father
lord over us,
the kingdom recedes
to the level of a mercenary province.
It smells of militias at every border.

Acids trickle into the ear
not of a lone, sad king,
but those of adolescent kings by the thousands,
of men who would be kings
without this poisoned rhapsody of lies.

But you already know, my prince,
that when southerly winds blow upon us,
cobwebs fly up
and as dark as everything around us may be
you can clearly see "the herons, the hawks."

Saxifrage

The saxifrage's lesson:
                    bloom
between rocks,
            be so bold.

Sueño

En el sueño había pájaros
pájaros encendidos para siempre
alegorías sin duda
y había un jardín radiante
aguaribay helechos casuarinas
contra la glacial certidumbre:

caminará por puentes,
nadará entre dos aguas,
sonriendo a piedras siempre ajenas,
entrará en el verano
como en prado de ortigas
sin más jardín que el de la noche.

2

Se le escapan las crines de las manos
desagua en la planicie se ve sola
disuelto como se borra la confianza
el torrencial caballo al fin de humo
que entre el viento la trajo
al borde mismo del derrumbadero
hasta este andén del ansia. Ya es el día.
En los sueños renacen los dilemas.

Dream

1

In the dream there were birds
birds aflame forever
doubtless allegories
and a radiant garden
pepper trees ferns casuarinas
against glacial certitude:

she will cross over bridges,
swim between two waters,
smiling at stones always out of reach,
she'll step into summer
like into a field of nettles
with only the night for a garden.

2

The mane slips from her hands
the plains empty of water she's alone
the way confidence is erased the torrential
stallion dissolved vapor after all
that brought her in the wind
to the very edge of the precipice
this antechamber of anxiety. Now it's day.
Dilemmas are reborn in dreams.

Unicornio

Tiene el narval la gloria de su cuerno
—torneada forma, insólito tamaño—
y la inquietud de sospecharse extraño,
sin saberse del cielo o del infierno.

Marfil en el rincón, color invierno,
en el museo erige hermoso engaño,
fraguando su leyenda año tras año
mientras albea el unicornio eterno.

Va el narval por el agua verdadera
sin que nadie se ocupe de su suerte.
Mientras, en aguas del soñar espera,

más firme, el unicornio milenario:
paladín de la luz contra la muerte,
invicto ante lo real, lo imaginario.

Unicorn

The narwhal has the glory of his horn
—extraordinary size, spiraled in shape, —
and the disquiet of suspecting himself strange,
without knowing if he's hell or heaven born.

Ivory and a beautiful deception adorn
this niche in the museum in winter shades,
forging his long legend through the ages,
while dawn-white shines the eternal unicorn.

The narwhal swims in waters that are true
and no one even looks after his fate.
Meanwhile, in waters that our dreams construe

the unicorn, more firm and millenary,
light's paladin against death, awaits:
unconquered by the real, the imaginary.

Parvo reino

1
Palabras:
           palacios vacíos,
ciudad adormilada.
¿Antes de qué cuchillo
llegará el trueno
—la inundación después—
que las despierte?

2
Vocablos,
vocaciones errantes,
estrellas que iluminan
antes de haber nacido
o escombros de prodigios ajenos.
Flota su polvo eterno,
¿Cómo ser su agua madre,
todavía una llaga
en que se detuviera,
pasar de yermo
                 a escalio
con su abono celeste?

3
A veces las palabras
entran en un acorde,
las cascadas ascienden,
rota la ley de gravedad.
Luna muy poderosa,
la poesía acoge desoladas mareas
y las levanta donde puedan
arriesgarse hacia el cielo.

Tiny Kingdom

1
Words:
        vacant palaces,
city half-asleep.
Before what knife
will the thunder arrive
—the flood follows—
that awakens them?

2
Vocabularies,
errant vocations,
stars that irradiate light
before their birth,
or debris from distant marvels.
Their eternal dust floats.
How to become their mother liquor,
even a wound
on which to pause,
how to go from arid
                        to arable field
with their celestial mulch?

3
Sometimes words
form a chord,
the waterfalls ascend,
break the law of gravity.
Poetry, a powerful moon,
gathers desolate tides
and lifts them up where they can
hazard the skies.

4
Campo de la fractura,
halo sin centro:
                    palabras,
promesas, porción, premio.

Disuelto el pasado,
sin apoyo el presente,
desmenuzado
el futuro inconcebible.

5
Prosa de prisa
para
        servir como de broza,
prosa sin brasa,
de bruces sobre
                    la página,
ya no viento,
                brisa apenas.
Temer su turbulencia
como el bote arriesgado
quien no nada.

4
Field of fault lines,
halo without a center:
                    words,
promises, portion, prize.

The past dissolved,
no support for the present,
crumbled
the inconceivable future.

5
Prose under pressure
used
        as deadwood
prose without live coals,
face down on
                the page,
no longer wind,
                    barely breeze.
Fear its turbulence
like one who can't swim
fears a reckless boat.

Prado para Orfeo

Ala toca la música la piel.
Entonces somos campos de la verdad,
ceremonia que sube
en un coral hermoso.

¿Demonio delirio es
o ángel obseso que cruza
con su espada de luz nuestros oídos
y nos lleva de vuelta, de vuelta
al paraíso,
al Éufrates eufónico?

Trompetas segurísimas bajan desde Tubal
y clavecines hubo
y el violín demorado
regresa a un amor de la infancia,
real de nuevo como el féretro blanco
y la campana.

Todas las lluvias, todas
las que cayeron en aquellas
esquinas, trasmanos y destiempos
no nos han empapado
como este Nilo,
esta frontera musical
que el alma
sólo ganando pasa.

A Meadow for Orpheus

Music, a wing, touches our skin.
Thereafter we are fields of truth,
a ceremony rising
in a radiant chorale.

Is this the demon of delirium,
or the obsessed angel that brushes
our ears with his sword of light
and takes us back, straight back
to paradise,
to the euphonic Euphrates?

Infallible trumpets descend from Tubal
and there were harpsichords
and the drawn-out violin
returning to a childhood love,
as real again as the white coffin
and the bell.

All the rains, all
that fell on those
corners, out of reach and ill-timed,
haven't soaked us
like this Nile,
the musical border
that the soul can pass
only by earning it.

Oscuro

Como este pájaro
que espera para cantar
a que la luz concluya,
escribo entre lo oscuro,
cuando nada hay que brille
y llame de la tierra.
Inauguro en lo oscuro,
observo, escarbo en mí
que soy lo oscuro
     hacia
lo más oscuro,
por el fondo del pozo
     del tiempo
del ser casi no ser,
tras la semilla, gema,
origen, nacimiento
     de mí,
de madre, abuelas,
inalcanzable océano
     de tiempo
y perdidas criaturas tragadas.

Mágico Patinir
     y perverso
gruta fuera del mundo.
Cree avanzar
el que rema en su fondo.

Dark

Like this bird
that waits until the light dies
to begin singing,
I write in darkness,
when nothing shines
and calls out from the earth.
I commence in the dark,
I observe, I burrow within myself,
as I am the darkness,
                        toward
what's darkest of all,
down the well
            of time
of being-almost-nonbeing,
after the seed, gem,
origin, birth
           of myself,
of mother, grandmothers,
unattainable ocean
               of time
and lost, swallowed-up creatures.

Patinir, magical
              and depraved,
his otherworldly cave.
The rower in the background
thinks he's making headway.

De tigre el salto

De tigre el salto,
de tigre, el emboscado escondrijo.
La Vida velocísima
                deja
tras el zarpazo,
el desgarrón por donde gotea
la constancia.

Luego vienen los argumentos del olvido;
mansos
lamemos la nueva cicatriz
cuando nos duele, oscura,
y olvidados del bosque,
otra vez lo cruzamos
por lo mínimo diario.

From Tiger the Leap

From tiger the leap,
from tiger, the ambushed hideout.
Life lightning fast
                    leaves,
after claws swipe,
the gash from which perseverance
drips.

Then come the reasons to forget;
tamed,
we lick the new, dark scar
when it aches
and oblivious to the forest,
we cross it again
for our daily minimum.

Dejábamos un ángel

Dejábamos un ángel feliz de nuestra memoria rodando
por la fecunda cascada. . .
para que la pasión con que aferramos
piedra, hoja, aun la espuma en lo hondo,
haga brotar cuando no estemos
una materia fervorosa, un hálito
estallante que no muera en la muerte,
un imán para nuestros fragmentos fantasmales
que huyen, huyen, huyen
sin que los fijen
los cuatro cabos de la fronda.

We Left an Angel

We left a happy angel from our memory swirling
in the fecund cascade. . .
so that the passion with which we cling to
stone, leaf, even foam in the depths,
can make fervent matter sprout
when we're gone, a burst
of breath that doesn't die with death,
a magnet for our phantasmal fragments
that flee, flee, flee
without them being tied
by the four ends of the bandage.

Translator's note: Opening lines in italics are from Álvaro Mutis's poem "El viaje" ("The Voyage").

No dicen, hablan, hablan

No dicen, hablan, hablan
"Quienes hablan no saben,
quienes saben no hablan."

Heraclitano fluir insiste:
"no saben, los incrédulos,
ni escuchar, ni decir."

La perfección acaso rige
la distancia que aleja
lo real palabra de lo real objeto.

Muere el mundo de olvido.
Puede en cambio repetir ferino
el plenilunio del error ajeno.

¿Poema o sólo cánope?
¿Verdad esplendorosa o recipiente
de vísceras ajenas?

Como sobre remordimientos,
por la inquietud, de constante olvidada:
¿es destino o es incauta deriva?

Un grave frío cruza el sentir
que se ha creído mágico:
su brasa no transmite, inútil.

Not Saying, Talking, Talking

Not saying, talking, talking
"Those who talk don't know,
those who know don't talk."

The Heraclitan flow insists:
"the skeptics don't know
how to listen or say."

Perfection may govern
the distance separating
the real as word from the real as object.

The world dies of oblivion.
In contrast, it repeats, ferocious
the full moon of another's mistake.

Poem or only canopic jar?
Splendorous truth or receptacle
for others' viscera?

As if beyond regrets,
because apprehension, forever forgotten:
is it destiny or reckless drift?

A dire chill cuts through meaning
that believed itself magic:
its idle ember conveys nothing.

Y entonces el techo no existe,
nos devuelve la noche de siglos,
el hueco terrible primero: el silencio.

Verano

Todo es azul,
   lo que no es verde
     y arde,
        I.N.R.I.
—*igne natura renovatur integra*—
en este aceite grave del verano;
cae el que pesa el vuelo de los pájaros
y blasfema del pájaro sin vuelo,
cae la excrecencia verbal =
                la agorería = el trofeo,
la joya sobre la vieja piel de siempre.

Quien se sienta a la orilla de las cosas
resplandece de cosas sin orillas.

And then the roof disappears,
restoring the night of the ages,
that terrible, first void: silence.

Translator's note: The title is from a line in Octavio Paz's poem "Pasado en claro" ("A Draft of Shadows").

Summer

Everything that's not green
   is blue,
      and burns,
         I.N.R.I.
igne natura renovatur integra
—through fire, nature is reborn whole—
in the summer's sober oil;
the one who weighs the flight of birds falls
and blasphemes the flightless bird,
verbal excrescence falls =
                    augury = trophy,
a jewel on the same old skin.

Whoever sits at the edge of things
is resplendent with things without edges.

Jardín de sílice

Si tanto falta es que nada tuvimos.
—Gabriela Mistral

Ahora
hay que pagar la consumición del tiempo,
sin demora,
            gastado el arrebato
en andar por un jardín de sílice.
Aramos otra vez el mismo surco
para fertilidad de la desdicha,
y la letra,
            el silencio
van entrando con sangre.

Años vendrán para pacer palabras
como pastos oscuros,
echar a arder pequeñas salamandras,
todos los exorcismos,
apenas memoriales donde hubo un aire libre,
ya no lugar común,
                        que nadie
en el miedo de las encrucijadas
sueña o lee.

Vagos vagones cruzan
                        hacia
un pasado que pulveriza las raíces,
que alisa el luto y nos despide.

Garden of Silica

If so much is missing it's because we had nothing.
—Gabriela Mistral

Now
the consumption of time must be paid for
without delay,
                    the rapture spent
strolling through a garden of silica.
We plough the same furrow again
for misfortune's fertility,
and the letter,
                    the silence
enter with blood.

The time will come for grazing on words
like dark pastures,
setting fire to small salamanders,
all exorcisms
meager memorials where wind once blew free,
no longer a commonplace
                         that no one
in fear of crossroads
dreams or reads.

Rambling train cars travel
                         toward
a past that pulverizes roots,
that smooths out mourning and dismisses us.

Sequía

De se taire, parfois, riche est l'occasion
      —Raymond Roussel

Y tienen las palabras su verano,
su invierno, y tiempos de entretierra
y estaciones de olvido.
De pronto se parecen demasiado a nosotros,
a manos que no tocan
hijos, amigos,
y pierden su polvo en otra tierra.
Ya no las mueve el agua
de nuestra tibia orilla humana.
Navegan entre nieblas,
merodean lentísimas,
van como topos, ciegas, esperando.
Hermanas, tristes nuestras.

La palabra

Expectantes palabras,
fabulosas en sí,
promesas de sentidos posibles,
airosas,
          aéreas,
                    airadas,
                              ariadnas.

Un breve error
las vuelve ornamentales.
Su indescriptible exactitud
nos borra.

Drought

On some occasions keeping silent is the best option
—Raymond Roussel (tr. Mark Ford)

And words have their summer,
their winter, and times of betweenland,
as well as seasons of forgetting.
Suddenly they resemble us too much,
or hands that don't touch
children, friends,
leaving their dust in other lands.
The water of our warm human shore
no longer moves them.
They sail in fog,
prowling ever so slowly,
blind, like moles, in anticipation.
These sad sisters of ours.

The Word

Expectant words,
fabulous in themselves,
promises of possible meanings,
artful,
        aerial,
                irate,
                        Ariadnes.

A slight error
makes them ornamental.
Their indescribable exactitude
erases us.

Guerra nocturna

toda la noche estuvo luchando ...

Vas subiendo lidiante una ladera
que enseñorea diego de la noche
pisas estribo sin estreno
trampa tendida trampolín
talco tibio del sueño sacudido
y fría tiza luego frío cristal
araña huraña luna sola remando por su niebla
el gato el gallo el golpe de la puerta.
Va el balde estrepitosamente al pozo.

Trastienda

Cielos veloces de Montevideo,
estratos de oro y de laurel,
halados por la más alta red,
tibios lilas lentísimos
cocientes de su luz multiplicada,
pasan y nos envuelven
y nos entretenemos con su gracia,
como una mano juega
entre arenas que guardan
la eternidad en la que no pensamos.
Entretanto, el pegaso peligro
relincha ferozmente.

Nocturnal War

all night he was wrestling ...

Struggling you ascend a slope
where beauty-of-the-night is lord
you step into untouched stirrups
trap set trampoline
tepid talc of the disrupted dream
and cold chalk then cold crystal
surly spider lonely moon rowing through its fog
the cat the cock the knock on the door.
Down falls the bucket with a clatter into the well.

Backroom

The swift skies of Montevideo,
stratus clouds of gold and of laurel,
drawn by the highest net,
tepid *lentissimo* lilacs
quotients of their multiplied light,
pass over and envelop us
and we amuse ourselves with their grace,
like a hand playing
in sands that safeguard
the eternity we don't ponder.
Meanwhile, the Pegasus peril
bucks fiercely.

Mujer con perro

Puedes andar lentísima, detenerte inexacta,
correr de nada a nada,
mirar lo absurdo, lo perdido, lo inútil,
coser a cada noche su frío,
introducir sílabas de estar viva,
de empecinada renaciente,
parecerte a ti misma.
Tu perro es tu testigo y tu constante huérfano.
Por él la soledad te privilegia;
se te admite un circuito ritual,
que traza, posiblemente atroz, el hábito.
Si él volara podrías ir subiendo
levemente en el aire
sin que ojo alguno te reclame.

Woman with Dog

You can walk ever so slowly, halt inexact,
run from nothing to nothing,
observe all that is absurd, lost, useless,
stitch some cold onto each night,
introduce syllables about living,
about obstinate rebirth,
resemble yourself.
Your dog is your witness and your constant orphan.
Because of him solitude privileges you;
you are allowed a ritual circuit,
atrocious perhaps, drawn up by habit.
If he were to fly, you could climb
lightly through the air
without a single eye to reproach you.

La historia no se olvida

El oropel del oro arrecia en las vidrieras,
a erizada distancia, en la ciudad extraña.
¿Cómo tener aquí sentido, nombre?
Huésped casual que apartó los aceites
sale a reclamar respuestas
de una extranjera superficie,
tan estrellada y negra, tan vacía;
torva que sólo abraza el desdén,
resbala entre la noche altiva y cae,
cae sin alcanzar tus hombros,
ahogándose en la ciudad
sin sal y sin gaviotas,
pero llena de espectros,
de dedos que se mueven con geranios,
tan cerca todavía debajo de la tierra.
Todo querría pisotearlo,
querría una rueda de fuego discerniente
que librara a los limpios.
De nuevo cierro el círculo,
salvos dentro unos pocos *anónimos*,
varios Velázquez, aquelarres Goyas
—esas serpientes tristes también mudaron piel
y apagaron los cielos aullando como lobos—
y más allá prosigo, ya sin país, los pasos.
La historia no se olvida y roe, roe.

History Is Not Forgotten

The glitter of gold intensifies in the windowpanes,
at a bristly distance, in this strange city.
How to have meaning here, a name?
Chance guest who separated the oils
sets out to exact answers
from a foreign surface,
so starry and black, so empty;
baleful, only embracing disdain
she slips in the haughty night and falls,
falls not reaching your shoulders,
drowning in this city
without salt or seagulls,
but full of specters,
of fingers that move with geraniums,
so close, still, beneath the earth.
I want to trample it all,
I want a ring of discerning fire
to liberate the pure.
Again, I close the circle,
safe inside a few Anonymous,
various Velázquez, Goya's witches' sabbaths
—those sad serpents also shed their skin
and blacked out the heavens howling like wolves—
and further on I resume, now stateless, my steps.
History is not forgotten and it gnaws and gnaws.

Capítulo

DONDE AL FIN SE REVELA
QUIÉN FUI, QUIÉN SOY,
MI FINAL PARADERO,
QUIÉN ERES TÚ, QUIÉN FUISTE,
TU PARADERO PRÓXIMO,
EL RUMBO QUE LLEVAMOS,
EL VIENTO QUE SUFRIMOS,
Y DONDE SE DECLARA
EL LUGAR DEL TESORO,
LA FÓRMULA IRISADA
QUE CLARAMENTE
NOS EXPLICA EL MUNDO.

Pero luego el capítulo
no llegó a ser escrito.

Chapter

WHERE AT LAST IT IS REVEALED
WHO I WAS, WHO I AM,
MY FINAL RESTING PLACE,
WHO YOU ARE, WHO YOU WERE,
YOUR NEXT DESTINATION,
THE COURSE WE TAKE,
THE WIND WE ENDURE,
AND WHERE IT STATES
THE LOCATION OF THE TREASURE,
THE IRIDESCENT FORMULA
THAT CLEARLY
EXPLAINS TO US THE WORLD.

But then the chapter
was never written.

Este mundo

Sólo acepto este mundo iluminado,
cierto, inconstante, mío.
Sólo exalto su eterno laberinto
y su segura luz, aunque se esconda.
Despierta o entre sueños,
su grave tierra piso
y es su paciencia en mí
la que florece.
Tiene un círculo sordo,
limbo acaso,
donde a ciegas aguardo
la lluvia, el fuego
desencadenados.
A veces su luz cambia,
es el infierno;
a veces, rara vez,
el paraíso.
Alguien podrá quizás
entreabrir puertas,
ver más allá
promesas, sucesiones.
Yo sólo en él habito,
de él espero,
y hay suficiente asombro.
En él estoy,
me quede,
renaciera.

This World

I only accept this illuminated world:
true, inconstant, mine.
I only exalt its eternal labyrinth
and its certain light, even if it hides.
Awake or between dreams,
I tread this weighty land
and its patience in me
is what blooms.
It has a soundless circle,
a limbo, perhaps,
where I blindly await
rain or fire
unleashed.
Sometimes its light changes,
and it becomes an inferno;
sometimes, rarely,
a paradise.
Maybe someone could
crack open doors,
see beyond
promises, successions.
I only dwell within it,
await it,
and that's wonder enough.
In it I am,
may I remain,
reborn.

Paso a paso

De pronto vendrá el viento
y será otoño.
Se va el verano
y cae algún recuerdo
y baja otro escalón
sin ser notada la vida,
de amarillo en amarillo.
Adiós, atrás,
el paso que no he dado,
la insegura amistad,
apenas sueño.
Será otoño de pronto.
No hay ya tiempo.
Perdí un mágico doble
de mi nombre,
un pasajero signo
que pudo hacer el mundo más exacto.
Perdí la paz,
la guerra.
Perdí acaso la vida
y acaso aún no gané
la propia muerte.

En el vacío espacio
alguien tañe una cuerda,
poco a poco.
Ya es otoño, tan pronto.
No hay ya tiempo.

Step by Step

All at once wind will come
and it will be autumn.
Summer leaves
and a memory falls
and life descends another rung
without being noticed,
from one yellow to another.
Farewell, behind,
the step I haven't taken,
friendship uncertain,
barely a dream.
All at once it will be autumn.
There is no more time.
I lost a magic double
of my name,
a passing sign
that could render a more exact world.
I lost the peace,
the war.
Perhaps I lost my life
and haven't yet earned
my own death.

In the empty space
someone plucks a string,
little by little.
It is autumn already, so soon.
There is no more time.

Final de fénix

No era verdad
el fabuloso vuelo
pero fingíamos creerlo
por casi hermoso.
La miramos llegar
a un cielo falso
subiendo su proclama
de oro en oro
en rosa sombría de teatro,
en inerte crepúsculo.
Seguíamos su vuelo
con ácida paciencia.
Pronto,
roído el día
por sus mismos vapores
fue cediendo
ante la noche limpia.
Aguardábamos
el fruto del incendio,
lo imprevisible
figurado en gloria.
Al cabo fue cayendo
hacia la tierra
entre sombras
de vuelos de ceniza.
Y no vimos batir
ala ninguna.

Finale of the Phoenix

The fabulous flight
wasn't true,
but we pretended to believe it
for being almost beautiful.
We watched her reach
a false sky
hoisting her proclamation
from gold to gold
to theatrical dusty rose,
to lifeless sunset.
We followed her flight
with acerbic patience.
Soon,
day corroded
by its own vapors
succumbed
to night's limpidity.
We awaited
the fruit of the blaze,
the unforeseeable
in figurative glory.
At last she slowly fell
toward the earth
among shadows
of ashes in flight.
And we didn't see
a single wing beat.

Encuentro y pérdida

Se va la tarde de hoy,
voy a perder las gracias ofrecidas.
La memoria entreabierta
señala una pradera fresca de tiempo antiguo
para por él hundirse,
para tornar por ella,
hacia la edad sin prisa ni cansancio,
despertarla, pedirle sus promesas,
recobrar mi alma dulce,
mi confianza,
el fuego aquél sin humo ni agonía.
Pero el atardecer llega
como lluvia total, a disolver
el tiempo en el que pude renacer
—o morir— hacia algo eterno.
Todo tiembla:
un último rayo de sol en las terrazas,
una isla de nube, un solo pájaro;
todo corre, se ordena, se concierta
en un signo preciso de abandono,
para apagar la fiesta aquí,
para ir más lejos,
a dar en otras manos las antorchas.
Todo estaba a mi alcance,
todo de pronto es nada.

Encounter and Loss

Today's afternoon is fading;
I will lose the loveliness offered me.
Memory half-opened
signals a cool meadow from ancient times
in order to sink through them,
in order to return through that place
to an age without hurry or weariness,
and awaken it, exact its promises,
restore my sweet soul,
my confidence,
that fire without smoke or agony.
But nightfall arrives
like an absolute rain, dissolving
the time when I could be reborn
—or die—on the way to something eternal.
Everything trembles:
a last ray of sun on the terraces,
an island of clouds, a single bird;
everything races, arranges itself, conspires
in a precise sign of abandonment,
to smother the festivity here,
to go even further
and pass the torches to other hands.
Everything was within my reach;
everything at once is nothing.

Sobrevida

Dame noche
las convenidas esperanzas,
dame no ya tu paz,
dame milagro,
dame al fin tu parcela,
porción del paraíso,
tu azul jardín cerrado,
tus pájaros sin canto.
Dame, en cuanto cierre
los ojos de la cara,
tus dos manos de sueño
que encaminan y hielan,
dame con qué encontrarme,
dame, como una espada,
el camino que pasa
por el filo del miedo,
una luna sin sombra,
una música apenas oída
y ya aprendida,
dame, noche, verdad
para mí sola,
tiempo para mí sola,
sobrevida.

Furtherlife

Give me night
the accorded hopes,
give me your peace no more,
give me miracle,
give me at last a parcel,
a portion of paradise,
your closed blue garden,
your songless birds.
Give me, the moment I close
my face's eyes,
your two hands of sleep
that guide and freeze,
give me a way to find myself,
give me, like a sword,
the path that follows
the sharp edge of fear,
a moon with no shadow,
music just heard
and already learned,
give me, night, truth
for me alone,
time for me alone,
furtherlife.

La noche, esta morada

e il naufragar m'è dolce in questo mare.
—Giacomo Leopardi

La noche, esta morada
donde el hombre se encuentra
y está solo,
a punto de morir y comenzar
a andar en aires otros.

El mundo va a perder nubes, caballos,
vacila,
    se asombra,
        se deshace,
cae como en los bordes del deseo
pero ya sin milagro.
Despacio la esperanza
viste su piel de olvido.
No veo más allá
de un nombre que he llamado
letra a beso a caricia
a rosa abierta a vuelo ciego a llanto.

Y como todo está desposeído,
todo con el pie justo
para tocar en tierra oscura,
el cielo vuelto un hueco sin voz
y sin orillas,
ya no soy yo la pobre,
medida entre mortales, melancólicos aires,
cuerpo cegado de luz o simple lágrima.
Lo que este mar, esta crecida sombra

Night, This Dwelling

and foundering is sweet in such a sea.
—Giacomo Leopardi (tr. Jonathan Galassi)

Night, this dwelling
where man finds himself
and is alone,
about to die and begin
to move in other air.

The world will lose clouds, horses,
it vacillates,
        marvels,
                dissolves,
falling as if on desire's edge
but now without a miracle.
Hope slowly
puts on its cloak of oblivion.
I can't see beyond
a name I've called
letter to kiss to caress
to an open rose to blind flight to weeping.

And as everything is dispossessed,
everything with the proper foot
in order to touch dark earth,
this sky turned into a hole without voice
or boundaries,
I am no longer the poor one,
measured in mortal, melancholic air,
body blinded by light or a simple tear.
What this sea, this swollen shadow

va perdiendo,
viene a salvarse en mí,
nube siempre,
caballo azul,
eterno cielo.

loses little by little
comes to be saved within me,
forever cloud,
                    blue horse
                              eternal sky.

Poems in Search of the Initiated: An Essay

During a time of impatient readers, poetic creation continues on, like a pleasurable mystery that resists resolution. Poetry, like death, perhaps, is surrounded by explanations. These explanations—diverse and insufficient—are justified, however, as being essential proof of the constant importance of that which, arising from a private occurrence, has had a public presence throughout time—which I now imagine redoubled by space.

What can be more private, more secret even, than the moment when a verse arises? When with that first mysterious coagulation, the rare phenomenon of the poem begins? This doesn't always occur, of course, because certain conditions are necessary so that the illumination doesn't dissipate and the momentary, propitious disposition can sustain that state without decay.

I don't believe any explanation of that strange process could satisfy us completely. Opposing critical camps coincide in omitting one. But there is still etymology—the only indisputable evidence. On the one hand, a mystery is whatever is secret, that which is reserved for the mystai, the initiated (who sometimes are more numerous than one thinks, and so my reference to space above). On the other hand, mystery implies ceremony, a service, which leads us to the idea of ministry. In both cases, it refers to an activity that, if not secret, at least is reserved for the few. But its ancillary function can, in the best of cases, result in service for the community.

Following Bernard Shaw's witticism, "a common language divides" those who employ the name of poetry with different conceptions of it, for different aims. Maurice Blanchot states, "Today the writer, believing he's descending to the underworld, is content with going out into the street." Koine awaits us in the street, with its own set of problems that generally has little to do with the precision of language—which should be the poet's concern—or with the transcendence of poetry, or with ethics, in the deepest and broadest sense of the word. It's also true that these problems, which should unsettle all of us, seem to have attenuated so much that fewer and fewer people occupy themselves with them. Perhaps it's this impoverishment of the field that makes those who are mindful worry about the current direction of poetry.

The inexplicableness of poetic riddles, the mystery that unsettles those habituated to demand simplification and ironclad passivity, tends to be labeled as hermeticism = rarefied poetry for the few, almost for specialists. From this perspective it's easy to suppose that the poet, thus stigmatized, covets isolation, amassing difficulties like blocks for a dividing wall.

What impatient readers stumble over—mystery, an object of faith in religious terms—for readers of poetry should be an object of poetic faith that allows them to think that the mysterious and the secret can be uncloaked; the harnessing of enthusiasm and a certain lyrical sense are enough for deciphering and comprehension. The challenges awaiting a less confident reader may include unusual verbal constructions, not worn out by use, and a richer vocabulary. These are not impossible to face. The pleasure of enthusiastic decipherment releases a mysterious energy that moves not only the pages of poetry, but also the world's great prose. If you allow me, I wish to recall "the white mystery" that Felisberto Hernández pursued, with his way of gazing slantwise at things, so he could read within them what was below, the uninferred relationships, that positive mystery that unleashes energies, tempts us to participate with lucidity, and is not rejected by reason.

It's possible that this white, unsettling dragon prefers the field of poetry to that of prose. The allusiveness, the metaphors, the nuances that abound in the former require more mental effort. Imagine the work gymnasts dedicate to their bodies to master them satisfactorily! Mastering that ambitious form of language also has its rewards.

—Ida Vitale

Translator's Afterword

> Open the wasteland word by word
> open ourselves and look to that meaningful aperture.
> —Ida Vitale, "Task"

Vitale has been writing poems for more than seven decades, from her first published collection in 1949 *La luz de esta memoria* (The Light of This Memory) to her most recent volume published in 2021, *Tiempo sin claves* (Time Without Keys). As a whole, her work constitutes one of the most significant and original intellectual experiences in Spanish-language literature that bridges the twentieth and twenty-first centuries. Vitale's lucid and challenging poems form a coherent and ever-expanding oeuvre that persistently seeks fissures in fixed structures of knowledge, in language and perception, and compels us to rethink and re-experience ourselves and the world we cohabitate through her words and silences.

Unlike many of her Latin American contemporaries whose poetics are associated, however reductively, with various trends and movements like the avant-garde, colloquialism, political poetry, (feminine) subjectivity, or eroticism, Vitale's singular writing—often described as "classic and modern"—doesn't fit so neatly into a single category. Her poetry arises out of the contemplation of the real that simultaneously activates a fundamental inquiry into the nature of representation through language, which shapes such contemplation. Her words are deliberate and exact, the result of careful pruning to achieve verbal economy, so that each relatively short poem belies its prismatic complexity. Without compromising precision, she embraces language's ludic possibilities: its rhymes, alliterations, puns, antitheses, and contradictions. Her poetry says the world anew while concurrently revealing itself as palimpsest, rich in intertextuality, tradition, and history, though here history fails in its attempt to encapsulate the past and so forever "gnaws, gnaws" ("History Is Not Forgotten").

Time is one of the central themes of Vitale's poetry: how it renders all things fragile and fleeting; how we as humans futilely try to fight against it with certainties, dogmas, and fixed identities. This stance, when "man" is "enough unto himself," she suggests, leads to existential ignorance, isolation, and violence: "alone / he readies his knife" ("Program"). Instead, by placing herself and her poetic subject "off to the margin" ("So-Called Life"), her poetry opens space and silence, accentuates gratitude, and offers aesthetic, intellectual, and ethical lessons for other ways of being present in the pulse of existence, whether through a sudden gust of air, fossil-filled rocks, or a simple greeting. Vitale's inquisitiveness and wonder touch diverse areas of knowledge, opening a vital "field of fault lines" that is only possible when thought and words are nomadic, free to follow their "errant vocations" ("Tiny Kingdom"). With playful erudition, she recovers fragments and voices and makes space for new ideas to dance and take flight.

Ida Vitale was born in Montevideo, Uruguay, in 1923, a country already distinguished at the time for many celebrated women poets, such as María Eugenia Vaz Ferreria (1875–1924), Delmira Agustini (1886–1914), Juana de Ibarbourou (1892–1979), and Sara de Ibáñez (1909–1971). She grew up in a culturally rich environment during a time of relative political and economic stability. Her family, of Sicilian origin, was secular and comfortably middle class. Vitale received a humanist education in the schools where her aunt, Débora Vitale D'Amico, was involved as founder or director. Vitale became proficient in French and Italian, and also took music classes and voice lessons outside of school. In 1942 she entered the Universidad de la República in Montevideo to study law. When the School of Humanities and Sciences was founded and began offering literature courses, she changed disciplines and discovered her first literary mentor, the exiled Spanish writer José Bergamín. Not long after that, the Nobel Laureate Juan Ramón

Jiménez included some of her poems in an anthology of young Latin American writers.

From the 1940s to the early 70s, Montevideo was buzzing with creative energy. Vitale collaborated closely with a vibrant cadre of other young writers, critics, artists, and intellectuals who sought to revolutionize the region's literature and culture. Named the Generation of '45 or the Generación Crítica (Critical Generation), the group included scholar Emir Rodríguez Monegal, writers Mario Benedetti, Idea Vilariño, Carlos Maggi, and Amanda Berenguer, as well as the famed theorist and cultural critic Ángel Rama, who became Vitale's first husband, and with whom she had two children, Amparo and Claudio. The Generation's cultural projects were diverse, cosmopolitan, and transformational, and Vitale was an active, central participant. During this time she published her first five volumes of poetry, most notably *Oidor andante* (Listener Errant, 1972), co-founded the cultural journal *Clinamen*, wrote incisive literary and cultural criticism for newspapers and journals, taught literature, and translated many plays, mostly from the French and Italian, for Montevideo's theatrical renaissance. Various opportunities abroad were impactful in her formation: a fellowship in France, invitations to serve on international literary juries, and participation in historic conferences in Cuba and the Soviet Union, where she forged connections with authors such as Julio Cortázar and Gabriel García Márquez.

Like most of her generation, Vitale closely followed the triumph of the Cuban Revolution in 1959, and her personal political leanings aligned with those of the Uruguayan Communist Party until the beginning of the 1970s. Unlike many writers, however, as Pablo Rocca writes in his bio-bibliographic chronology of the poet, she "always rejected the synonymy of art and politics or placing art at the service of any cause." With the 1973 coup d'état and the start of the military dictatorship of Juan María Bordaberry, Vitale and her second husband, the Uruguayan poet Enrique Fierro, went into exile. From 1974 to 1984 they lived in Mexico City where

Vitale made lifelong friendships and resumed her multifaceted literary work: she taught at the prestigious Colegio de México, published translations and literary criticism, wrote for the journals *Plural* and *Vuelta*, both founded by Octavio Paz, and co-founded the newspaper *unomásuno*. Her first volumes of selected poems correspond to this period, as well as the rich *Jardín de sílice* (Garden of Silica, 1980). After the fall of the dictatorship, Vitale and Fierro returned to Montevideo where she directed the cultural section of the weekly *Jaque*. In 1990, the couple moved to Austin, Texas where Fierro worked as a professor. Vitale left Austin after her husband's death in 2016, and now resides in Montevideo once again.

While in Austin, Vitale published numerous collections of poetry that the present volume draws most heavily from, including *Sueños de la constancia* (Dreams of Constancy, 1988, 1994), *Procura de lo imposible* (Search for the Impossible, 1998), *Reducción del infinito* (Reduction of the Infinite, 2002), *Trema* (Trema, 2005), *Mella y criba* (Knick and Sieve, 2010), and *Mínimas de aguanieve* (Specks of Freezing Rain, 2015). Her literary project grew with marvelous works of prose, such as the hybrid work *Léxico de afinidades* (Lexicon of Affinities, 1994, 2006); a novella in poetic vignettes, *El ABC de Byobu* (2004; Byobu, tr. Sean Manning, 2021); an autobiographical account of her years in Mexico, *Shakespeare Palace: Mosaics de mi vida en México* (Shakespeare Palace: Mosaics of My Life in Mexico, 2018, 2019); and an imaginative bestiary on plants and animals in literature, *De plantas y animales* (2003). She also continued to actively contribute to cultural journals like *Letras Libres*.

As Vitale approaches her hundredth birthday, her lifetime of literature has gained long-deserved international prominence. In the last decade, several translations of her books have come out in French, Italian, Portuguese, and English; important compilations of her work have appeared across the Spanish-speaking world; and several critical studies of her work have been published, as well as a volume of her own literary criticism. A feature-length documentary of her life in twenty-six chapters was made in 2020. She has also accepted innumerable international invitations to read, and a stream of awards in Europe and Latin America: a doctorate Honoris Causa from the Universidad de la República (Uruguay, 2010), the International Octavio Paz Poetry and Essay Prize (Mexico, 2010), the Carlos Monsiváis Prize for Cultural Merit (Mexico, 2010), the Alfonso Reyes International Prize (Mexico, 2015), the Reina Sofía Prize for Ibero-American Poetry (Spain, 2015), the Federico García Lorca Poetry Prize (Spain, 2016), the Max Jacob Prize (France, 2017), the Guadalajara International Book Fair Prize (Mexico, 2018), the Delmira Agustini Medal (Uruguay, 2019), the Grand Prize for Intellectual Labor (Uruguay, 2021), and the rank of Commander of the Order of Arts and Letters of France (2021). Most notable of her accolades, perhaps, is the 2018 Miguel de Cervantes Prize (Spain), the highest award given in Spanish letters, for which she was the fifth woman recipient since its inception in 1976. In 2019 the BBC named her one of the world's 100 most influential women.

I met Vitale in 2000, before this whirlwind of recognition, or "Idamanía" as it has been called, really started to grow. As a doctoral student at the University of Texas at Austin in Hispanic literature, I wrote my dissertation on the poetry of Alberto Girri and Rafael Cadenas—the latest recipient of the Cervantes Prize (2023)—under the direction of Enrique Fierro. My friendship with both of them has become an immeasurable gift. Some of my fondest memories with Vitale from that time are brisk walks and long pauses to observe sparrows taking puddle baths and grackles congregating in trees; leisurely phone calls that usually began with the question, "What are you reading these days?" and ended with a long list of authors I urgently needed to explore; and a night of poetic magic when she and Fierro baptized my new dog, Juan Rulfo. I was honored when she asked me to translate her first collection in English *Reason Enough* (Host Publications, 2007), a selection drawn from *Oidor andante*. As when I translated that book, Vitale invited my questions while I worked on *Time Without Keys*. She and her daughter Amparo Rama generously clarified references and gave invaluable insights into the complex constellations of her poetic universe. As an accomplished translator of some thirty writers from Molière, Brecht, Genet, and Pirandello to Bachelard and Supervielle, Vitale has a particularly deep understanding of the art, and her own meditations on translation were welcome accompaniment during my labors. In the poem "To Translate," for instance, she suggestively writes that even when a "sentence […] reaches the lair / of formidable meaning," it is always already "disrupted within," a paradoxical necessity for the continual nomadic movement of the poetic word.

This *Selected Poems* has been carefully culled from Vitale's many poetry books, which themselves have undergone various groupings and revisions over the decades. The Spanish originals are principally taken from the most complete volume of her work, *Poesía reunida* (1949–2015), edited by Aurelio Major and published by Tusquets Editores in 2017. That volume arranges her texts in reverse chronological order, with the most recent poems first and the oldest ones last. As Major says, this logic governs her earlier compilations and reflects Vitale's constant displacement of limits while emphasizing her "cautious trust in the future, a duty to faith." We decided to follow the same overall structure for this edition, while the selection process involved making my own list of "classics" and asking Vitale and Major to send me their own favorites. This book attempts to honor the breadth of her themes, the range of her style and poetic forms, and the diverse registers of her diction, while privileging more recent poetry that had never appeared in English. In the end, Jeffrey Yang, the indefatigable editor of this book, helped with the difficult task of making the final cut from Vitale's seventy-plus years of poetry.

"Tell us how you feel to be turning 99," I asked Vitale in October 2022, just before she blew out the candles on an exquisite cake during a week of celebrations in Mexico City, one month before her actual birthday. "Coraje!" she laughed, without skipping a beat, choosing a word in Spanish charged with multiple meanings: anger and outrage, resourcefulness and courage. Her precise and witty response encompasses a continual commitment to contest "the fabricator's artful lies" ("Recalcitrant"), to unflinchingly observe men's long history of "savagery, maybe worse" ("Nostalgia for the Dodo"), to embrace the exhausting but urgent task of dwelling "among uncertainty" ("In the Dark Entryway"). It also encapsulates a lifetime of daring to "bloom between rocks" ("Saxifrage"), "to be human and woman, no more, no less" ("Fortune"), to "write in darkness / when nothing shines" ("Dark"). May we all be as courageous as her words.

—Sarah Pollack

Ida Vitale was born in Montevideo, Uruguay in 1923. She is one of Latin America's most celebrated and respected poets, and her writing spans over seven decades. Vitale has published over thirty works of poetry, prose, and literary criticism, in addition to numerous translations. In Uruguay, and later in Mexico, where she lived in exile, she was an important intellectual figure in groundbreaking cultural projects. Vitale was the fifth woman to win the Miguel de Cervantes Prize, the highest accolade in Spanish letters, and she has also been awarded the Reina Sofía Prize, the Octavio Paz Prize, the García Lorca Prize, and the Max Jacob Prize. In 2019, the BBC named her one of the world's 100 most influential women.

Sarah Pollack is an associate professor of Latin American literature and translation studies at the College of Staten Island and the Graduate Center, CUNY. Her prose and poetry translations from Spanish to English include works by Juan Villoro, Silvia Eugenia Castillero, Alain-Paul Mallard, Fabio Morábito, Enrique Fierro, and Ida Vitale.